PRAYING HOME

PRAYING HOME

THE CONTEMPLATIVE JOURNEY

Robert Llewelyn

Kallistos Ware

Mary Clare, SLG

COWLEY PUBLICATIONS

CAMBRIDGE, MASSACHUSETTS

Published in the United States of America
by Cowley Publications.

International Standard Book No.: 0-936384-52-2

The cover illustration is "Road to the North"
by Nora S. Unwin
Used by persmission of the Sharon Arts Center.

Library of Congress Cataloging-in-Publication Data

Llewelyn, Robert, 1909 -
    Praying Home.

    Bibliography: p.
    1. Prayer. 2. Contemplation. I. Ware,
    Kallistos,
1934 - . II. Mary Clare, Mother, S.L.G.
III. Title.
BV210.2.L55   1987   248.3   87-
20194
ISBN 0-936384-52-2

Cowley Publications
980 Memorial Drive
Cambridge, MA 02138

CONTENTS

PRAYER AND CONTEMPLATION
Robert Llewelyn
Prayer as Petition   1
A Difficulty Considered   5
Intercession and Miracles   12
Four Preliminaries to Contemplation   19
The Divine Office and the Jesus Prayer   26
The Cloud of Unknowing   33
The Cloud of Forgetting   38
Contemplation and Healing   42
Some Practical Points   47
The Practice of Contemplation   54
Epilogue   59

THE POSITIVE ROLE OF DISTRACTION IN PRAYER   61
Robert Llewelyn

THE POWER OF THE NAME   71
The Jesus Prayer in Orthodox Spirituality
Kallistos Ware

PRAYER: ENCOUNTERING THE DEPTHS   99
Mary Clare, SLG

INTRODUCTION BY RACHEL HOSMER

A generation or two ago in Anglican and Roman Catholic circles, contemplative prayer was regarded as the privilege of an elite, and to aspire to it prematurely was severely discouraged by spiritual directors and religious superiors. Spirituality was often described in terms of ascent, with beginners, for whom vocal prayer was appropriate, at the bottom. A middle group, called "proficients" or "advancing souls," came next, and were taught to master some of the recognized methods of meditation and affective prayer. The transition to contemplation involved two stages, the "prayer of simplicity" or "simple regard," which was attainable after a suitable preparation and purification in the lower stages, and the infused gift of contemplation proper. This final stage was out of the reach of ordinary folk, bestowed by God according to the divine pleasure.

How different is the situation today! Now we see a surge of interest in spirituality in our time, when people of all sorts—young and old, women and men, folks new in the faith as well as experienced believers—are looking for, finding and working with, the disciplines of a deeper, simpler form of personal prayer. Those who are looking for contemplative practice draw their nourishment from a wide spectrum of spirituality, East and West, traditional and brand new. Techniques from the ancient Fathers of the desert, the monastic writers of the middle ages and of our own time, mingle with TM, Hindu, and American Indian traditions and nourish, instruct, and admonish these new seekers for

God. This series of meditations written from within the Christian tradition, from Anglican and Eastern Orthodox perspective, is addressed to them.

The first and second pieces are written by an Anglican, Robert Llewelyn, from the perspective of Western spirituality. Without separating himself from the richness of Orthodox spirituality, he bases his work upon the *Cloud of Unknowing*, a fourteenth-century work by an unknown English author. Llewelyn begins, as Origen did in the second century, with an apologetic for prayer, especially for the prayer of supplication, which was the Lord's own prayer. Then he leads us into the Cloud author's recommendations for contemplative prayer. Llewelyn is writing to those readers who want to be taught the method of the Cloud, which is that of a prayer without words or images for God. From his own experience as a spiritual director, and from such writers as de Caussade as well as from contemporary works by Teilhard de Chardin, C.S. Lewis and Morton Kelsey, Llewelyn interprets this form of contemplative prayer and its disciplines for readers in the world of today. He provides a place for us to meet him with our questions, and helps us confront and respond to the realities within ourselves, both negative and positive, as we work with *The Cloud of Unknowing*. He helps us see how to return to our daily work and relationships with a fresh love, humbled, simplified, and strengthened bit by bit, through our openness to God and our perseverance in this prayer. One of his special strengths is the way he is able to help us make good use of problems, like the well-known "wandering thoughts." He makes the traditional distinction between voluntary distractions, which weaken prayer, and involuntary ones, which can be used to strengthen it. If they are accepted as the work of the Spirit, they may suggest a shift in imagery which can help us locate some hidden obstacles to grace of which we were not aware. Moreover, involuntary sleepiness in prayer is nothing to worry about. God loves us when we are asleep as well as when we are awake!

In the third essay Kallistos Ware introduces us to one of the most ancient forms of Christian contemplative prayer, the "prayer of the heart," and in doing so provides us with a rich background from history and Eastern Orthodox spirituality. He also gives us much practical help in understanding and practicing this prayer. Writing from an Eastern Orthodox point of view, he addresses religious, clergy and lay people alike, for whom the "Jesus prayer," one form of the "prayer of the heart," is a common daily discipline, not a special gift for a chosen few. This prayer–"Lord Jesus Christ, Son of God, have mercy on me, a sinner,"–was introduced to English and American Christians in a little book called *The Way of a Pilgrim* by an unknown Russian monk. It was translated into English by an Anglican priest in England, A.M. French, and presented to an American readership in 1931 by Bishop George Craig Stewart of Chicago. I remember being its read aloud in a convent in Boston in the early thirties, and wondering what my response should be to its demands which seemed to me excessive? How could I pray all the time? How could I say the same formula over and over, all the days of my life and at the same time concentrate on my work, my response to others, and the ordinary tasks of life?

Kallistos Ware's essay is helpful in answering just such questions as mine. He points out that this form of the Jesus prayer is only one of many ways for entering the "prayer of the heart." Earlier writers had suggested using short repetitive verses form the psalms, or the invocation, "O God, make speed to save us," and the like. Father Kallistos also emphasizes that not all of the laborious methods recounted in *The Way of a Pilgrim* are helpful for everyone. What counts is not the number of repetitions of the prayer, but a gentle consistent effort to remain *in* prayer, seeking to move first from the prayer of the lips to the prayer of the mind and finally to the prayer of the heart. The Jesus prayer, or our chosen psalm verse, may simplify itself as we persevere and even become a single word, "Jesus", or "Lord."

The last movement of the prayer, as well as the most difficult, is the descent "from the mind to the heart." Father Kallistos likens this inward movement to the slow spreading of a drop of ink falling upon blotting paper. It reminds me of another image from a tract on the Jesus prayer, which likens it to a drop of oil falling upon a woolen garment, permeating it with its fragrance.

The last essay is by an enclosed nun, also an Anglican, and formerly Mother Superior General of the Sisters of the Love of God, at "Fairacres" in Oxford. She begins her reflections with some theological considerations, and by defining prayer, and describes both prayer in community, "shared prayer," and solitary prayer. Like the authors she quotes–Augustine, Julian of Norwich, Thomas Merton–she describes the development of prayer as a movement towards the center, an encounter with the Holy Trinity. When encounter brings about in us *metanoia*, conversion, and its fruits of love, it attests to the reality of our prayer experience. Mother Mary Clare also speaks of a "nomad mentality," which she sees as a disposition to flee from the artificialities and complexities of contemporary life to simplicity, authenticity and freedom. She discards the idea that contemplative prayer is an advanced technique for the elite.

It is legitimate to ask whether an enclosed nun can have anything to say to active men and women in the world today. Her daily regimen, relationships, and responsibilities differ so much from our experience that one wonders whether there can be any real communication between us. Many people who visit monastic houses, however, have discovered that beneath the regimen which is specific to enclosed religious there is real fulfillment of a universal human need for order and discipline, as well as a deeply healing and nourishing atmosphere of serenity and simplicity.

There may be specific situations and forms of human suffering which enclosed celibate women are unqualified to deal with except through simple friendship and prayer; neither such friendship nor such prayer is inconsiderable.

We are all made in one image and the root of suffering in all human life is the same. A mature religious has been trained for and consecrated to a life of prayer; her very distance from some of our preoccupations may give her a helpful perspective on our deepest needs and aspirations, our common longing for holiness. Mother Mary Clare shows us that the encounter with God in the depths is no lily-picking affair, but a deadly conflict with the forces of evil within our hearts. Through that struggle emerges a sense of God, the living God, who is present to us.

American readers will be aware of the use of non-inclusive language throughout this book. It is significant, I think, that the essay by Mother Mary Clare—in which the use of non-inclusive language is the most pronounced—is the earliest in the collection. She wrote it in 1973; "man" is used throughout, without apology. Robert Llewelyn, writing in 1980, apologizes for speaking of God as "him" by saying in a parenthesis: let the personal pronoun stand. If you will edit the book for yourself in this respect as you go along, you will find yourself included and recognized, as well as fed.

Rachel Hosmer, OSH

PRAYER AND CONTEMPLATION

ROBERT LLEWELYN

PREFACE

Mystical experience is given to some. But contemplation is for all Christians. Allow me to say a word about that prayer which is needed for all of us ... [It] means essentially our being with God, putting ourselves in his presence, being hungry and thirsty for him, wanting him, letting heart and mind and will move towards him; with the needs of the world on our heart. It is a rhythmic movement of the personality into the eternity and peace of God, and no less for the turmoil of the world for whose sake, as for ours, we are seeking God. If that is the heart of prayer then the contemplative part of it will be large. And a church which starves itself and its members in the contemplative life deserves whatever spiritual leanness it may experience.

This passage from Bishop Michael Ramsey's *Canterbury Pilgrim*, (1974, pp. 59-60) conveys very well the general sense in which the word 'contemplation' is used in this book. In that sense it is, I believe, an experience into which every committed Christian may at some stage expect to be drawn. A growing number of people today are looking to the Churches—and often beyond—to lead them to a new dimension in prayer. These pages are written in the conviction that the key to their search lies within the great tradition of Christian spirituality, and in the hope that many will find in them the encouragement and guidance which they seek.

ROBERT LLEWELYN

CHAPTER 1

Prayer as Petition

I PROPOSE to approach our subject from the angle of *supplication*, a word which describes prayer in all its petitionary and intercessory aspects. Supplication is basic to the very idea of prayer—the etymology of the word *prayer* alone suggests that—and it is, I believe, the way most of us come to prayer, and an indispensable form of it in one way or another throughout our lives.

When the disciples asked Jesus to teach them how to pray he gave them as their model a prayer which is petitionary in form from beginning to end. It is true that it is placed in the setting of adoration, as all supplication to God should be—the first request is that God's name be kept holy. And it is true that the petition is never for selfish personal ends—the corporate aspect of the prayer is safeguarded throughout by the first two words, 'Our Father', reminding us that we make our petition as members of a family, regarding the needs of others with as much concern as our own. It is true, further, that our Lord's prayer lifts our sights far beyond our own small concerns, whether individual or corporate, beyond the horizons of family or community or parish or church or even nation. 'Thy kingdom come', we pray, 'thy will be done, as in heaven so on earth', thus projecting our desires to Ireland, to the Middle and Far East; to Russia, South Africa and all oppressed peoples; to India and the third world where poverty and destitution bring men and women to the brink of despair; as well as to our own country where the corroding power of affluence and greed is a constant threat to that foundation on which all true religion rests, the sense of trust and hope in God.

There is nothing parochial in petitions such as these. They embody the aspirations of very many people at this time, including those who

1

are out of touch with any form of organised religion, that the love of God which is at the heart of the gospel committed to us shall find its due expression in political, social and economic justice. Only when these great issues have been commended to God are we allowed to look to our more immediate needs, 'give us this day our daily bread', still praying as members of a family—for 'us', and not for 'me'—and asking for all things temporal and spiritual to enable us to fulfil God's purpose. We pass on to ask for the forgiveness of our sins, a petition which concerns our relationship with God as well as with one another; and then to the last petition, in which we ask God not to allow us to be tried beyond our strength and to save us from evil in the testing fire of temptation. The Lord's Prayer is thus petitionary throughout. The apparent exception—the doxology—is of course not part of the original prayer, but an addition used by the early Church.

★   ★   ★   ★   ★   ★

If we pass on from the Lord's Prayer itself to our Lord's direct teaching on prayer we shall find that it is always the petitionary aspect of prayer which is expounded. In St Luke's gospel the Prayer is immediately followed by the parable of the householder who, on the untimely arrival of a guest, goes at midnight to a friend's house to beg for food, and refuses to allow any peace to the man or his family until this request is granted. The almost parallel story of the unjust judge also urges us to persist in prayer. This time we have a widow pestering a judge until he attends to her needs and grants her the justice she is seeking. In the further parable of the pharisee and the publican it is once again petitionary prayer that is commended, the publican's cry that God will be merciful to him as a sinner. So too, in our Lord's most commonly quoted teaching on prayer, 'Ask, and it shall be given you, seek, and you shall find, knock, and it shall be opened to you', petitionary prayer pure and simple is placed before us. After being reminded that God will give not less lavishly and lovingly than a human father, we are led to the climax that God will surely give the Holy Spirit to those who ask him.

When we turn from our Lord's teaching to consider his own prayers as they are recorded in the gospels, we find that these too are basically petitionary. He prays for the soldiers, 'Father forgive them, for they do not know what they do', and for Peter, 'I have prayed for you that your faith may not fail'. He prays for the disciples, 'that they may be sanctified through the truth', and for the members of his Body, 'that they may all be one, even as, thou Father, art in me and I in thee, that they also may be one in us'. Finally we may recall the distress and anguish in Gethsemane, 'Father, if it be possible let this cup pass from me', leading on to petition at its most costly and sacrificial level, 'nevertheless, not my will but thine be done'.

What is true of the gospels is no less true of the epistles, where petition remains at the heart of prayer though, here too, purged of its selfish elements and ennobled by the fire of the Spirit. As an example of the grandeur and nobility to which such prayer may rise, let us take this passage from the Epistle to the Ephesians:

I bow my knees before the Father from whom every family in heaven and earth is named, that according to the riches of his glory he may grant you to be strengthened with might through his Spirit in the inner man, and that Christ may dwell in your hearts through faith; that you, being rooted and grounded in love, may have power to comprehend with all the saints what is the breadth and length and height and depth, and to know the love of Christ which surpasses knowledge, that you may be filled with all the fullness of God.

It is the same with the Old Testament. The commentaries, of course, tell us that prayer in the Old Testament can be understood widely to include every form of address to God, whatever its character—and this is strictly true. Yet, with two exceptions only (the Prayer of Hannah and the reference at the end of Psalm 72 to 'the prayers of David the son of Jesse'), wherever the Old Testament uses the word prayer, it is the petitionary aspect that is referred to. It may be that, unthinkingly, we often limit petitionary prayer to such passages as the description of Solomon's prayer at the dedication of the temple, or Nehemiah's at its re-building after the exile. We overlook the petitionary nature of such well-known sentences as 'O Lord open thou our lips', or, 'O God make speed to save us'. It may surprise us to learn that in Psalm 119 alone there are no fewer than seventy petitions to God.

3

Is the point I am making, that prayer in the Bible is deeply rooted in petition, an academic one only? If I believed that I would not have laboured it. On the contrary, I believe it to be a point of immense practical importance, for it seems that here nothing less than personality in God is at stake. Once the concept of petition at the heart of prayer is surrendered, it will not be long before we relinquish the idea of God as personal—and that is a statement which could equally well be put the other way round. The conceptions of God as Father and of prayer as petitionary are no more separable than the two sides of a coin. In parenthesis let me add that I am conscious, even as I use the word, that to speak of God as 'personal' is deplorably inadequate. I should prefer to use some such word as 'supra-personal', but I can no more conceive what that means than I can conceive of a fourth dimension or a beginning and end of time. We call God 'He'—and 'She' would do just as well, because the pronoun is used to denote person and not gender—not in the sense in which we use 'he' of a friend, but because the limitations of language leave us with the personal pronoun as the only alternative to 'it'. If God were 'IT', with capital letters—the greatest, so to speak, of all possible 'its'—we should be his master and not he ours. 'He' can do no more than indicate that God has the power of initiative no less than we have, even though we may believe that he has vastly more. The doctrine of the Trinity, in itself a mystery, encourages us in the belief that a concept of the Godhead beyond the personal as we know it, is not without meaning.

But to return to our argument. Once we lose the concept of personality as applied to God it will not be long before we lose the concept of him as 'absolute demand' and so of ourselves as owing him 'total commitment'. That is probably the danger of what is generally called mystical religion when it is divorced from biblical theology. This can be seen in the East, where the biblical insights we have just been considering are largely foreign. It can be seen too in some of the esoteric cults springing up in the West today, orientated around some *guru*. The practice of religion becomes a matter of preference, like the choice of friends, and there is lacking the note of urgency, still more of obligation which is stamped on the prophetical and dominical approach. I do not of course mean to belittle mystical prayer—the faithful practice of

4

silence, adoration, petition, may ultimately lead us into such prayer—
but simply stressing the importance of basing our prayer on firm biblical foundations. Thomas Merton once wrote: 'The simplicity of the
gospels, if kept in mind, makes false mysticism impossible. Christ has
delivered us for ever from the esoteric and the strange. He has brought
the light of God to our own level to transfigure our ordinary existence.'

CHAPTER II

A Difficulty Considered

READERS of this book will probably fall into two main groups. There
will be those who conceive of God in terms which deny personality,
regarding him (let the personal pronoun stand) as a sort of diffused,
impersonal, spiritual energy pervading the universe. It would seem to
follow that for such people prayer, as we have been regarding it, can
have no place in their lives. They might perhaps hope to *use* God, that
is to say, to harness this vast source of spiritual energy for the benefit of
themselves and others; but to beseech him, to appeal to him, to invoke
him—that would make no sense at all. You can harness the power of
steam and use it for the propulsion of ships and trains, but you cannot
address to steam the desires and aspirations of your heart.

The other group will include those of more or less orthodox Christian belief, people who affirm personality in the Godhead and who
pray to God as Father. Yet amongst these it may be assumed there will
be some who can find no place for petitionary prayer except, perhaps,
as allowing a certain psychological benefit to those who know they are
being prayed for. Having in mind the difficulties of this class, let us go
on now to consider the objection they are likely to bring against petitionary prayer and, as we proceed, some of the values conserved in this
realm of prayer may become clearer.

The objection would, I think, run on some such lines as these: 'I believe God to be perfect wisdom and perfect love. If he is all-wise he knows what is best. I should not like him to give what is second best, whether for myself or for anyone else, and if I prayed to him, I might be asking for just that. And anyway, if he is all-loving, surely he will give what is best without my asking him? Therefore I prefer to worship him, and to praise him, and to enter into silent communion with him, but not to ask him for anything, whether for myself or others. I leave it to him to give as he sees best.' This seems at first sight a not unreasonable argument, nor is it one presented exclusively by lukewarm or shallow people. It was, for example, one of the points held against Madame Guyon in her examination by the Roman Catholic Church, that her system of prayer allowed no place for petition or intercession.

The fallacy of the argument is that it considers only two possibilities: either God wills it, and therefore it will happen anyway; or else God doesn't will it, and therefore I must not pray for it—and presents them as a reason for not praying. But the argument has overlooked a third possibility, namely, that God may want this event to happen—this sick person, let us suppose, to recover—*in answer to our prayer*. Our line of reasoning has lost sight of the possibility that prayer may open a channel through which it becomes morally possible for God to work— as Father Raynes of the Community of the Resurrection used to say— not *changing* God's purpose, but *releasing* it.

The thought will be made clearer if we transfer our attention from the realm of prayer to that of action. Here then is a mother with her baby boy whose life depends on being fed at her breast. She reasons thus: 'God wants my child to live or he does not. If he wants him to live he will live anyhow, and I need not feed him. If he doesn't want him to live, it would be wrong of me to feed him. Either way I need do nothing,' The fallacy, painfully obvious in the realm of action, seems often to go undetected in the realm of prayer. God wants this child to live *through* the mother's co-operation, with all that this means to mother and child in establishing a relationship of dependence and love on which the healthy spiritual and psychological development of both depend. No basic change of principle is involved in God's dealing with men when we move from the sphere of action to that of prayer.

A DIFFICULTY CONSIDERED

What has perhaps been unduly laboured here is summed up tersely by C. S. Lewis as follows:

'Praying for particular things,' said I, 'always seems like advising God how to run the world. Wouldn't it be wiser to assume that he knows best?' 'On the same principle', said he, 'I suppose you never ask the man next to you to pass the salt, because God knows best whether you ought to have salt or not. And I suppose you never take an umbrella because God knows best whether you ought to be wet or dry.' 'That's quite different', I protested. 'I don't see why', said he. 'The odd thing is that He should let us influence the course of events at all. But since He lets us do it in one way, I don't see why He shouldn't let us do it in another.'

Whether it be odd or not, it is certainly beyond dispute that God does allow us to direct to some extent the course of world history by our hands and feet and brains, these physical organs being but three among many which, as instruments of the human will, may influence the stream of events around us. When the atom bomb was dropped on Japan in 1945, bringing the war abruptly to an end, every country in the world felt in some measure the impact of that event. And God allowed this to come about through man—man's brain in designing 'that hideous strength', and man's body acting in co-ordination with his mind and will.

And yet, while it is true that God allows man an astonishing degree of freedom in shaping events for good or ill, that freedom is by no means absolute. Limitations are placed upon it—not necessarily for all time, for the domain under man's control progressively increases as nature yields up one secret after another. Where this will stop we have no means of knowing. Man can modify the weather by planting trees or cutting them down, or by firing chemicals into rain clouds, but he cannot control it to any extensive degree. Man can regulate the birth rate, but the sex of the unborn child is not—as yet—within his power to decide. Nor can he command the ebb and flow of the ocean tides. It is easy to see how human control over such things could lead to disaster, and we may be thankful that God in his wisdom has placed them, and much more besides, beyond our present powers. Yet these, and other examples we might take, serve to remind us of the astonishing range of freedom which he does allow.

If then, we may ask, God entrusts so much to us through the exercise of free will in the realm of action, would it not be strange if he should entrust nothing to us in the realm of prayer? We do not find any such division between action and speech—doing things and asking things— in ordinary family life. Each has its part to play in developing and deepening relationships in the home. The child will at one time express his heart's desire by action—playing cricket in the garden, romping with the dog, or making a model aeroplane—and at another time he will express it by speech, asking his father if they may go camping for the summer holidays this year. The father will not always agree to the boy's request, but it is through the expression of the will in action and speech that family relations are enabled to grow.

Our Lord encourages us to look to the family if we would discover the manner of God's dealing with us, and nowhere is this more true than in the realm of prayer. Surely it is just what we should expect— that the relationships proper to normal family life should have their counterparts among us who have received the spirit of adoption whereby we cry, 'Abba, Father'. It is the plain teaching of Jesus, that God our Father, in his love for us, wants us to look to him to supply our needs, whether temporal or spiritual, with the simplicity and faith of children, and to make known our requests boldly. It is true that he knows our needs before we ask him—we have our Lord's word for that— but prayer will prepare us to receive his gifts and use them in his service. Fellowship and communion will be taken to new depths and—a mark always of true discipleship—our lives will be irradiated by a spirit of thanksgiving.

To make a request to God in prayer does not mean that we are excused from working as far as we are able to bring about the end for which we have prayed. If we pray, 'Create in me a clean heart O God and renew a right spirit within me', we must order our lives as far as possible to that end. The way we live will be the test of the reality of the way we pray. The example chosen is a prayer for spiritual blessing, but prayer for material blessing is equally enjoined in the New Testament. Not only does our Lord teach us to pray for material blessings, but it is to such prayer that he responds in his healing miracles and he continues to confirm his teaching in the experience of men and women throughout the ages and not least in our own time.

★   ★   ★   ★   ★   ★

What then am I saying—that we may pray for whatever we want? We are certainly free to *take* all our desires to God in prayer. It may be that he will grant them, even when the things we seek are not what we might call his primary will for us, as a father might decide to allow a head-strong schoolboy son to be out at night even though he knew the boy's best interest (and thus his own primary will) lay in his remaining indoors and doing his homework. The Bible expresses that thought in Psalm 106, 'Lust came upon them in the wilderness and they tempted God in the desert. And he gave them their heart's desire and sent leanness withal into their soul.' Colin Morris has expressed it still more tersely in the words, 'Look out what you pray for—you may get it', adding that, to judge from the mess we are in, many people's *real* prayers—meaning by 'real prayer' the heart's desire and not necessarily the utterance of the lips—have indeeed been granted.

If, however, we are trying to be realistic and sincere in our Christian living, our basic desire will not be that God should bend his will to ours, but that through the discipline of prayer our wills may be brought into closer conformity with his—that he will cleanse the defective desires of our hearts by the inspiration of his Holy Spirit. This, for the committed Christian, is a continuing process, and he knows that, at each stage, what he looks to God to give him is likely to fall short of what God would have him receive, and so every prayer he makes is governed by the petition, 'thy will be done', whether explicitly expresssed or not. This means that we are prepared—or at least desire to be prepared—for anything, even if God's plans should drive a deep furrow across our own. The anonymous writer of the following words must have been well schooled in God's way of dealing with his people:

> So easily do we pray for the wrong things: for strength that we may achieve, and God gives us weakness that we may be humble; for health that we may do great things, and God gives us infirmity that

we may do better things; for riches that we may be happy, and God gives us poverty that we may be wise; for power that we may have the praise of men, and God gives us weakness that we may feel the need of him; for all things that we may enjoy life, and God gives us life that we may enjoy all things; and so, receiving nothing that we have asked for but all that we have genuinely hoped for, our prayer has been answered and we have been blessed.

Although often we shall not know how to pray as we ought, we shall naturally seek to avoid what may be called the forbidden areas of prayer. Prayers which often seem permissible when we view ourselves or others in isolation may become impossible when we reflect that we pray as members of a family in which the good of one may conflict with the interest of another. It is also important that our prayer shall specify 'open possibilities'. Here we are in some difficulty, but in practice all of us recognise that God has so ordered the world that some situations are open to prayer and others are closed. For example, most Christians would think it right to pray for a friend with a septic arm, presuming the situation to present an open possibility. If the arm had to be amputated, we should say God had declared himself (in respect, at least, of his permissive will) and our prayer would be directed to our friend's mental adjustment to his new state. But it isn't always easy to know what is open and what is closed. Sickness, for example, we should generally hold to be open; the weather some would probably regard as open and many as closed; the timing of the ebb and flow of the tides we should all regard as closed. But it is important to note that closed possibilities exist not because God's power is limited, but because, if the world were otherwise organised and disciplined, life as we know it would become impossible.

Considerations such as these show petitionary prayer to be a very different thing from what people out of touch with the Church sometimes *imagine* Christians believe it to be—a sort of Aladdin's lamp which we can so manipulate as to bring about our fondest wish. If that picture were to bear any resemblance to truth, the only condition under which chaos would not immediately ensue, would be if the lamp itself were in the hands of infinite wisdom and perfect love. and while it would be misleading to press the rather crude comparison any further—for God is a master lover, not a master magician—that is just where we would claim the lamp to be. At the same time, belief in God's sovereign control does not exclude the possibility of his allowing man a certain freedom in the realm of petitionary prayer—a freedom consistent with human love and wisdom indeed, but consistent also with God's power to say 'no' as well as 'yes'.

I find it much easier to understand the man who denies absolutely the existence of God than the man who, believing in the God and Father of our Lord Jesus Christ, makes him deny us any active co-operation with him in the realm of prayer. That prayer *does* effect new things—that certain events which would not otherwise have happened do happen as a result of prayer being offered—Christians must surely believe beyond all doubt. Yet, as we have seen, we need to balance this insight with another. We do not go to prayer that we may use God but that he may use us. We trust him to use our prayer as he wills in the extension of his blessing, and we trust him further to make us, through the discipline and training of prayer, more effective instruments of his will. One result of prayer will be to make us more fit to receive aright the good things, spiritual and material, which God wants to give. And prayer for one another will build us up into a fellowship of love, the deepest of all blessings, from which much else will flow.

CHAPTER III

Intercession and Miracle

INTERCESSORY prayers such as we are familiar with in church have both advantages and dangers. The advantages, as has well been said, are their theological depth and richness, their spiritual insight, their balance and beauty of language and their range, so far beyond what our own prayers are likely to compass. They give us a standard to which we may increasingly approximate, setting before us things of lasting value in place of the transient things on which we so easily set our hearts. But these are values into which we have to grow. 'When I use the Church's prayers', says Colin Morris, summing it all up in one colourful sentence, 'I feel like a small boy wearing his father's suit, hoping he will grow into it one day.'

But prayer is never just a matter of words. Its roots are in the desires of the heart. The act of speaking may often assist us in developing and expressing our inmost desires, but the words are a help to *us*, not to God. We should be warned also that words and phrases, however holy they may sound, cannot become prayer merely by being repeated. For prayer requires always an involvement of mind and heart and will, and wherever this is present in relationship with God, there will prayer be offered, whether words are said or not. Conversely, no verbal utterance without such involvement can be of the nature of prayer at all. When Christians pray as they are taught, 'Thy kingdom come', it may be that only for the saints of God are words and desires perfectly blended into one. For most of us, the words will express not so much our desire as it is as, rather, what we desire that it shall be. We desire indeed that God's kingdom shall come, but we do not desire it with the whole of ourselves. If when we pray we put the energies of our spirit, fervently yet unaffectedly into our words, then the words will help to kindle our hearts and bring utterance and desire into harmony. There is a danger, however, that words, instead of being an expression of the interior

12

energies of the spirit may be used as a substitute for it. If so, they become a mockery—'vain repetition', as the Authorised Version has it in a pregnant phrase. People sometimes think that vain repetition means, simply, saying the same prayer over and over again. But this need not be so; the Jesus Prayer, for example, is a form of prayer which lends itself to continuous repetition, but it is far from being on that account vain. The reality of a prayer has nothing to do with the number of times it is repeated, but depends rather on the simplicity and truth in which it is made. A prayer repeated only once, if the heart is not engaged, is a vain repetition.

However helpful it may be to use words in intercessory prayer, we do well to remind ourselves they are not of its essence. We are familiar enough with this in everyday life. Collectors for charities do not usually speak to passers-by—holding out the box is itself a sufficient request. Suffragettes who chained themselves to railings knew that actions speak more eloquently than words. Equally, we may intercede by asking God to accept this or that activity as a prayer for the cause we have at heart. This is no soft option—it is, in fact, as costly as we choose to make it. Thus one person may get up early to make his Communion on behalf of a sick friend; another may do some piece of work; others again may deny themselves some pleasure or luxury, or make an offering of money to some representative cause—the possibilities are endless. There is no need to keep the friend or the cause in mind throughout such times, a simple act of intention is enough, together with an offering of heart and will to God of what we have chosen to do.

Commenting on Hebrews 7:25, 'He ever lives to make intercession for us', Bishop Michael Ramsey has said that the basic meaning of intercession is not pleading with God but standing in God's presence on behalf of another. And so, simply to hold another in the silence before God, may become for us the most important way of intercessory prayer. On such prayer John Austin Baker has an illuminating passage in his book *The Foolishness of God*:

> When we pray for others we shall see that by far the most important requirement is inner calmness and tranquillity. We are not engaged in creating or producing anything, but in becoming aware of what is

already the fact, namely that God is immediately and intimately present both to ourselves and to the one for whom we are praying. Our task is to hold the awareness of this in the still centre of our being, to unite our love for them with God's love, in the quiet but total confidence that he will use our love to help bring about the good in them which we both desire. In technical terms, therefore, intercession is a form of that kind of prayer known as 'contemplation', with the special feature that here we contemplate not God in himself but God in his relationship of love to those whom we also love; and on the basis of our partnership with him we entrust our love into his hands to be used in harness with his own for their benefit.

★　★　★　★　★　★

It has been said earlier that many people would be prepared to defend prayer only at what might be called the psychological level. They would say, for example, that John's knowledge that Paul is praying for him in his sickness will be a comfort and strength, and an assurance that he is loved and cared for. Probably they would add that this knowledge might help John towards a new hope and courage, which in turn would be likely to react upon his bodily condition, so that the prayer offered would indeed assist his return to health. Certainly no Christian would be concerned to deny that this is one of the ways in which petitionary prayer acts. Nor, if he is wise, will he belittle its importance. But he will be bound to admit that to restrict the operation of prayer to some such mode as this fails completely to do justice to the teaching of Our Lord and of the New Testament as a whole, to the witness of the early church and indeed to the Church's experience in every age, including the present. When Our Lord said to blind Bartimaeus, 'Receive your sight', or when St Peter said to the cripple at the gate of the temple, 'In the name of Jesus Christ of Nazareth stand up and walk', we are in the presence of a new creation—what takes place can in no sense be explained subjectively within the terms of raising a man's morale. We are in the presence of a miracle.

I think it ought to be said that belief in miracle does not mean we believe that God, in answer to prayer, will suspend or change natural laws on which the orderly ruling of the universe depends. If a child were to fall over a precipice the natural result would be for gravity to pull him to the ground. But if his father by an act of will stretches out his hand, grabs his son and pulls him back to safety, no one imagines the law of gravity to have been susupended—we simply recognise that a new force, projected into the situation, has had its way. So too, when our Lord walked on the water there was no suspension of the law of gravity, but a new power was interposed by the divine will. The point is expressed as follows by Bishop Reichel (quoted in A. L. Worlledge's book, *Prayer*):

> The intervention of the divine will in answer to prayer, by simply directing the energies and powers of nature to a result which, if left undirected, they would not have arrived at, seems to me, on the most careful reflection, just as possible as that of which we see the results in every part of the globe at every moment—I mean the intervention of the human will, not in the way of 'suspending' or 'superseding', but in the way of using the laws of nature by directing natural forces into certain channels.

We note that the quotation begins with the words 'the intervention of the divine will', and it is that which is always the essential element of miracle. In his booklet, *Our Understanding of Prayer*, the late Bishop Ian Ramsey of Durham makes the same point, though rather more cautiously, in these words:

> Prayer undoubtedly supposes that it makes sense to speak of God's activity as directed to a particular point and as effecting something new in the universe. Does it? We all know how human effort can change the world and how by thought and skill we can create novelty in town and country. It is true that in our case this needs the intervention of our bodily organism. But if God is related to the whole universe in the way described earlier—on the analogy of ourselves to our bodies—this may still be a profitable reflection. In general terms we are only required to believe in principle that God can act within the texture of the universe, and certainly the Christian can have no fundamental difficulty with this concept. The Christian certainly

15

cannot in principle exclude God's special activity in Christ from being effective in nature and human nature.

In his book *The World and God* another writer, Dr H. H. Farmer, lists three elements which he holds to be indispensable to miracle:

First, there is an awareness of serious crisis, or need, or threat of disaster in the personal life, and of helplessness to deal with it adequately and victoriously through the exercise of ordinary, unaided powers. Second, there is a more or less conscious and explicit turning to God for assistance. Third, there is an awareness of an *ad hoc* response to God, to the situation and to man's petitionary inadequacy in it, so that the crisis is met, the need satisfied, the danger averted in an event, or combination of events, which would not have taken place had not man so petitioned and God so acted.

Miracle then involves a special breaking in of God to the world, and in the sense in which Dr Farmer uses the term, this comes about in answer to man's prayer. We have ordinarily no means of knowing how often this may happen, or indeed, when it does happen that it has done so in answer to some specific prayer—God, after all, does know our needs before we ask him. But for my own part I do not require proof in order to believe that we are covered with divine or angelic protection much more frequently than we are likely to be aware.

I do not know how well-known is the following story about the beloved Bishop of Lincoln, Edward King, but I tell it as I remember hearing it from a younger member of the family. The Bishop was walking alone one night along one of the lonely fen roads outside Lincoln to visit a sick person to whom he had been called. When he arrived at the cottage he found no one ill, nor could anyone explain the message. The matter might have ended there but, some years later, a condemned murderer whom the Bishop had prepared for confirmation told him that it was he who had sent the message, that he had been lying in wait in the ditch to assault and rob him, when he had seen to his surprise that the bishop was not alone but was flanked by a man on either side.

Even a Christian so much aware of spiritual realities as Bishop King would have remained unconscious of divine protection but for this unexpected sequel; and there may still be left in the story an element unrevealed—a prayer offered specially for the Bishop's safety. If we go strictly by Dr Farmer's definition some such such petition would seem necessary if we are to call the episode a miracle. But in my view it is miraculous as it stands. We do not know just how God may have protected us, not only—or even chiefly—from bodily harm, but from spiritual dangers which might have quite overwhelmed us, nor to what extent other people's prayer may have been instrumental in this. No doubt the visible evidence of angelic protection such as this story illustrates is of rare occurrence, but it is legitimate to wonder how much of what we generally call coincidence, or chance, or luck, may not be due to a special providence of God.

★ ★ ★ ★ ★ ★

The question naturally arises that if God can, and often does, intervene, why does he not do so more often? What are we to make of the car accidents, the plane crashes, the tragic shootings and the whole field of disaster with which our papers are so largely filled, as well as the daily onset of fatal illness and sudden death? No definite answer can ever be given to such questions, but there are certain reflections that have to be made.

The first of these is that God did not intervene to save his own Son from suffering and death on the cross, though he might have done so. Even after the decisive victory of Gethsemane, Jesus is fully aware that the way of deliverance is still open. 'Do you think', he asks the soldiers who arrest him, 'that I cannot appeal to my Father and he will at once send me more than twelve legions of angels?' But that appeal was never made. The really breathtaking aspect of God's love in the Incarnation is the self-emptying and humiliation, leading to the anguish of Gethsemane and Calvary where our Lord took on himself all the suffering man can experience, and more. The theoretical problem of suffering may remain, but in the power of the Spirit it is seen to be transcended and taken into the redemptive purpose of God. A Christian sees God working from within every tragedy and occasion of suffering which, in union with Christ, become experiences that are redemptive for the world itself.

Brother Edward, pioneer of the Village Evangelists, expresses this in one of his letters:

> I do seriously believe that all suffering patiently endured is linked with the one suffering of Christ in redeeming the world. I believe that if I can suffer bravely and put faith and courage and love into it, that suffering of mine will count towards the world's salvation. I believe that actually those who suffer in the Spirit are, under Christ, our greatest and most generous benefactors. They do more for us than the busiest who bustle about in service.

A further reflection is that there must be, in regard to God's special intervention, a great economy of action. If God were to interfere in every situation where we got ourselves into difficulties, all controlled, disciplined and planned life would be at an end. If no fire broke out when the children upset the oil stove, if the aircraft didn't fall when the mechanic had failed to tighten a vital nut, and if the same absence of risk were to be found in every department of life, there could be no incentive to carefulness, responsibility, order, discipline. Moreover, every future event would be unpredictable, and planning, in any free human sense, impossible. It is because we are set in a framework of natural law which normally goes unhampered on its own majestic course, that life as a school and training ground for character can exist at all. If life were studded with miracles comparable to the stilling of the storm and the feeding of the five thousand, man, at his present stage of moral development, would be lost. When these things happen once or twice in a lifetime, they serve to reveal the autonomy of God's creative power and to awaken adoration and trust. When the Queen visits a school a week's holiday is given. The school can absorb that because there is only one queen and she is not likely to return in the next hundred years—no school could survive a monthly royal visit and no economic system could survive a frequent multiplication of loaves.

Yet as a final consideration, can we be sure that we ought to wish for miracles even if we saw them as possibilities? Many people think of miracle as a reward of man's faith. We forget it may equally be a concession to his weakness. The stilling of the storm is just such a case. Our Lord's primary will for the disciples was not that they should be spared the ordeal of the storm, but that they should meet it with untroubled hearts, in serenity and trust. Hence he rebuked not merely the winds and the waves, but the panic-stricken men whose faith had failed. Those who have grasped the values and priorities of the kingdom will know that its deepest rewards are found where troubles, distresses, calamities, disappointments—whatever form the storm may take—have been accepted and passed through lovingly and trustfully in God's saving grace. This does not mean that God's succour, in whatever way it is present, is not to be accepted. It would be presumption on our part to think we know best how our deliverance should be brought about, but the whole tenor of the New Testament is that we should normally expect deliverance *through*—and not *from*—trial and affliction. The reward for the man who has built his house upon the rock of the gospel is not that it shall be protected from the batterings of nature but, that after the rains have fallen and the floods have risen and the winds have blown, it shall remain firm. In the words of Mother Julian, 'He said not *thou shalt not be tempested* but *thou shalt not be overcome*'.

CHAPTER IV

Four Preliminaries to Contemplation

THE FIRST POINT, which governs all that I shall have to say, is that life must be taken and accepted as a whole, and prayer can never be separated from life, except for the purpose of analysis. Of course, a good deal depends on how we define prayer. Some people speak of prayer as if to equate it with Christian living. Their way of praying, they would say, is caring for old people or visiting the sick in hospital. If we choose to enlarge our definition of prayer in this way we must allow it also to include washing-up and gardening, earning a living and travelling to work, doing the crossword, eating, drinking and sleeping. The whole

19

range of life will be included. And we should indeed be on shaky ground if we were to claim greater value in the sight of God for any one of these activities rather than another; for the value of any work resides not in the nature of the work itself, but in the love which inspires us to respond to God in whatever he calls us to do. In *The Practice of the Presence of God*—a little book but a great spiritual classic—Brother Lawrence saw, with true insight, how all perfection could be contained in such a simple act as picking up a straw off the ground, if only it were done solely for the love of God. Such an action would be a purer form of prayer than the performance of some work beneficial to society but lacking the motivation of love. *Though I give all my goods to feed the poor, and though I give my body to be burned and have not love . . .*

Now whilst I am fully prepared to go along with this view which sees prayer as co-extensive with Christian living, and to agree further that in holding it one holds also to some important principles—it does away, for example, with a false antithesis between secular and religious— yet clearly it is not a view of prayer which will serve my purpose in writing this book. For by adopting it I should commit myself to writing on the whole range of Christian life rather than on one specific activity within it. In the following pages we shall be regarding prayer as the activity in which we are engaged when, alone or in company with others, our hearts and minds and wills are occupied with God and with him alone; and we shall regard all other activity, whether 'religious' or 'secular' as the overspill of that prayer into the daily life of the Christian. God is to be glorified in the whole of our life, but this is only likely to happen if we ensure that there are regular times in which we seek him and only him, times in which every motive other than the glory of God is, as far as may be, excluded. God does not value our prayer time because it is in itself more valuable than other times, but because the other times should be charged with the significance of this particular time. The point has been well summarised by John Dalrymple in his book *The Christian Affirmation*—'You are never likely to be able to pray everywhere all the time', he says, unless you first learn to pray somewhere some of the time.'

But in so limiting the activity of prayer we must remember that it is never to be disengaged from the total offering of life. It is the risk that this may happen—and in fact sometimes does—that has so often brought the subject of prayer into disrepute. And so we must stress like a thread that runs through all our thinking, the principle that prayer can never be sealed off in a compartment on its own. Prayer and life will be continually acting and reacting on one another. Insofar as our daily work is not open to the impulse and direction of the Holy Spirit, to that extent will our prayer life be weakened; and conversely, insofar as there is a holding back or want of openness in our prayer life, to that extent will the work we offer to God be enfeebled. Dedication in our prayer life without a corresponding dedication in our work can be no more than an appearance—it is our work that tests the reality of our prayer. Naturally it will take time for prayer to permeate the whole but ultimately, all aspects of life will move towards a deeper consecration, each supporting and encouraging the other.

★ ★ ★ ★ ★ ★

The second point which underlies all that we shall be saying is that only the Holy Spirit can teach us how to pray. That is so obvious as to be almost trite—we hear it again and again, we meet it in all the books and, perhaps for just that reason, we pay it less attention than we should. We can of course find help and direction from books and from people, but in the end, prayer is the work of the Holy Spirit within us and he alone is our teacher. The Spirit, says St Paul, comes to the aid of our weakness. We do not even know how we ought to pray, but 'the Spirit himself makes intercession for us with groanings that cannot be uttered'. Here perhaps we are coming close to a definition of contemplative prayer—'Groanings which cannot be uttered', 'sighs too deep for words' (in the RSV) or, in the paraphrase supplied by one of the commentaries, 'inexpressible longings which God alone understands'. Contemplation is indeed a gift, the gift of the Spirit which only he can impart and only he can develop within us. It should be sought by waiting rather than by effort, gently, and with a patience that abides God's time rather than urging our own desires. The Spirit moves where he wills, and whether he moves us to pray vocally, to 'speak with tongues' or to be silent in contemplation, he alone is our teacher and guide.

PRAYER AND CONTEMPLATION

Many years ago when I was about twenty-four, I remember going for
a walk with Father Wigram, the Superior at that time of the Cowley
Fathers at St Edward's House in Westminster and a man of considerable
spiritual stature. Bede Frost's book, *The Art of Mental Prayer*, had
recently been published and was enjoying a good deal of popularity. At
the heart of the book there are descriptions of the various methods of
meditation—the Oratorian, Carmelite, Ignatian, Franciscan and others. I
should be unable to say much about them now, but I had read the
book at the time and no doubt said a good deal. We were nearing the
end of our walk when I turned to my companion and said, 'And Father,
how do you pray?' A few moments' silence and then he said, 'Well, I
usually kneel down and hope for the best'. It was a rebuke I well de-
served, though not perhaps intended as such—the saints have a way of
making devastating remarks with artless simplicity. To kneel down and
hope for the best is good advice if we see hope as a theological virtue,
along with faith and charity, the confident expectation that God the
Holy Spirit will complete within us the good work he has begun. And
with every period of prayer this process is carried forward. It has taken
me many years to learn to kneel down and hope for the best. Let us not
forget the place of freedom and simplicity in prayer.

★　★　★　★　★　★

But to say that is not to imply that prayer, like every other activity,
does not have its own technique. And here is the third point I wish to
make. The word 'technique' may seem an inappropriate one to apply to
prayer, but the fact that it can be misused should not deter us from
securing its proper use. People sometimes say, and especially nowadays
when *gurus* are being increasingly sought out in the western world, that
prayer is some form of technique. That is an error as far, at least, as
Christian prayer is concerned, and needs to be refuted. But the place of
technique within the life of prayer is quite another matter and one we
should be foolish to neglect. The end of prayer is encounter with the
living God—communion, or fellowship, as we may equally call it—and
technique must always be subordinate to encounter. As I write these
words I am hoping for encounter—I hope that my spirit may commune

with my readers' spirits and to that end I must use a technique, in this case, that of writing words in the English language.

A few years ago I was asked to give a talk to some Sisters in a convent in France. They knew little English and I knew less French and so, as the technique was poor, the encounter was spoilt. Of course there is a difference when it is God we are speaking to, for God looks not at the outward forms but at the heart and thus the outward forms, of which language is one and posture another, become matters of indifference. So I think we must say that technique is important from *our* point of view, but not from God's. Have you ever watched yourself or a friend speaking on the telephone? We nod our head up and down, shake it from side to side, we may clinch a point by making a gesture with our free arm—all of which may look a bit foolish since we are speaking to someone who cannot see us, but is both reasonable and sensible if it enables us to communicate better. So too, if technique helps us to pray better, there is no reason to despise it.

Later we shall enquire how technique relates to posture, and the correlation between tension and relaxation in different parts of the body. More attention has been paid to this in the non-Christian East than in the West. The truth is that you can approach a matter of this sort in two ways. Take, for example, the relationship of sleep to posture. Suppose you are out for a picnic and you fall asleep, your body will at once take up a posture suited to sleep— horizontal on the ground. But you could also start from the other end and say to yourself, 'Now that I want to go to sleep, I shall first lie down on the ground and then, given the desire for sleep, it will soon overtake me'. You have the same choice in prayer—in contemplative prayer the body will tend to assume the posture best suited to that state, but equally, if we consciously take up the position most conducive to prayer then, as prayer is what we intend and want, prayer will come. To many people that may sound artificial and mechanical applied to prayer. Yet every night, in regard to sleep, we first take the correct posture and then let sleep overtake us— and there is no difference in principle between the two. Of course the Holy Spirit alone can enable us to pray, but that need not prevent our taking a posture which will assist his action in us. There is still, it is true, the danger of mistaking the outer form for the inner reality but this can be overcome if we are alert and ready for it.

★   ★   ★   ★   ★   ★

As my fourth and final point in this chapter, I want to stress the importance of regarding prayer as an offering. This is especially true of the prayer of praise and thanksgiving, and of waiting upon God in silence. The psalmist says, 'I will offer unto God the sacrifice of thanksgiving and will call upon the name of the Lord.' The same thought is given a Christian content by the author of the Letter to the Hebrews who writes, 'Through Jesus let us continually offer up to God the sacrifice of praise, that is, the tribute of lips which acknowledge his name.' Our offering in prayer is to be linked with the offering of Jesus, in virtue of which we are reconciled to God, and so may offer ourselves as sons to their Father. We are enabled to make this offering not of ourselves but through the prevenient action of the Holy Spirit. Yet the offering *is* ours, for God does not override our freedom—it is ours as a response to grace, gladly and freely given. And since it is made through Jesus, we shall find encouragement in remembering that it cannot be made on its own, but is a part of the total offering of his mystical body the Church.

If we are able to see prayer quite simply in this way, as an offering, one important consequence will follow. We shall be relieved of all anxiety to make a 'success' of prayer, whatever that may mean. This in turn will save us from the discouragement which is perhaps the commonest reason why people do not persevere in their life of prayer. What we are doing in silent prayer often appears at the time to be futile and, since this *is* only an appearance, one of the soundest pieces of advice for anyone who is finding prayer difficult is, never to judge by how it seems to be at the time but only—if at all—by its later fruits. If our whole concern is to offer our prayer to God, we need not bother with the questions that arise in our minds—'Is this prayer helping me or anyone else? Is it strengthening? Is it helping my troubled mind and emotions?' Ignore such thoughts. Offerings were never meant to help or strengthen or do anything except be offered. We leave our offerings confidently and lovingly in God's hands; we do not demand that this or that should come of them. If we can offer our prayer with this kind of simplicity we shall be delivered from the one great enemy of prayer, subjectivity—those sideways glances at ourselves to see how we are getting along—and our lives will come to be more and more deeply rooted and grounded in God. We have already seen how praying and doing react upon one another and so, of course, what has been said about offering applies also to our daily work. The important thing about work is not that it should be a 'success' but that it should be whole-heartedly offered, and it will be helpful to recall that thought from time to time. But I believe we are likely to see this dimension of our work only if we are learning to see it in our prayers.

Offerings can, of course, go wrong. Some time ago a family in India sent me a gift of sweets. It came out of a background of poverty we in the western world would find hard to imagine, and when the parcel reached me the contents were spoilt and had to be thrown away. But the value of the offering, lying not in the substance of the gift but in the love which prompted it, remains unchanged. So with our prayers— of little worth in themselves, they are yet accepted for love's sake. These are very simple thoughts, but we cannot be too simple before God, and if we keep them in mind we will be helped by them.

Some people, however, are worried by this idea of prayer as offering—it suggests to them the picture of an eastern potentate delighting in the homage of his subjects. But that is a false picture and a quite arbitrary one, for God is not to be compared with an oriental monarch but with a father. A father takes delight in his child's offering not because it inflates his ego but because, through the total action, the relationship of father and son is enlarged and enhanced and it is in this progress of love that the father rightly delights. Father Benson of Cowley once wrote,

> God appointed prayer . . . not because he had any delight in our formal homage but because he desired, by forming in us the habit of prayer, to draw us to look to himself, the fountain of all good.

As John Macquarrie has said in his book *Paths in Spirituality*, 'The glorification of God and the sanctification of man are not competing motives in worship.' And he quotes St Irenaeus as presenting in a few

words the paradox which is always present in the situation of worship:
'The glory of God is a living man; and the life of man consists in
beholding God.'

CHAPTER V

The Divine Office and the Jesus Prayer

WE ARE perhaps accustomed to think of contemplative prayer as
belonging to those times when we kneel or sit or stand in silence in
the presence of God. Certainly the heart's silence is of the essence of
such prayer, but this does not necessarily mean the absence of words,
and there will be many times when the recitation of the divine office or
some other form of vocal prayer, such as the rosary, will reveal themselves as contemplative in nature. Often, for example, in saying the
psalms of the office we may be drawn beyond the words to the very
heart of prayer, our attention no longer on the words but on God
himself. Father Augustine Baker, the seventeenth-century author of
Holy Wisdom, a classic of spiritual direction, says that vocal prayer was
'ordained to this end, to supply and furnish the soul that needs with
good matter . . . by which it may be united to God'.

The words of the office thus become the framework of our prayer
and are there to support us when we need them. Here is a simple
illustration. As I look out of my window, I see a large and rather old
pheasant on the lawn. It runs gaily along the ground, takes a short flight
and then, being tired, returns to the earth; then a little more running,
another flight, and so on. It occurs to me that the recitation of the
office can be rather like that. We move steadily along from verse to
verse of the psalms, and then there may be a short period, as it were on
the wing, when the words, though still recited, recede into the background and we are somehow taken beyond them and held for a few

moments in that stillness which is God. And then—and this too is the point—just as our pheasant had the good solid earth to return to and support him as he moved forward again, so we have the words of the office to return to and be our support. The bird could not just fall into a void, and in the same way the words of the office prevent us falling back into the distracting and discordant imagery which often holds our minds.

We might well have approached the office from another angle. Indeed, it would have been more natural to do so. I have not because I wished to show how the office might be a way in to contemplative prayer—little bursts of it like the bird's little bursts of flight. But before the office does this for us, the repetition of its words, with due attention paid to them as the Spirit empowers us, can be a tremendous help in enabling us to collect our minds, and to leave behind the distractions and concerns and perplexities of life which so often scatter our mental and spiritual energy. That is primary for all of us, and if I did not mention it first it is because I assume we can understand it for the purposes of our present discussion.

It will help to make what I am saying more clear if you will picture to yourself three parallel horizontal lines. The middle line stands for the words of the office. The line below stands for the distracting occupations of daily living from which the words of the office, acting as the agent of the Spirit, continually draw our minds upwards; while the top line stands for contemplative prayer where the Spirit will at times take us beyond the words into the stillness which is God. Note that we are taken; we do not make the leap ourselves. It just happens as we go on our way, while the words remain to support us as we may need them.

Yet we have to be realistic and say that for one reason and another the daily office has largely dropped out of the worshipping life of the Church and that the opportunities which were open to people of an older generation are less often available today. There are encouraging signs of a renewed desire for this aspect of the Church's worship and perhaps the situation will change again. Meanwhile what I have said is not wasted because the underlying principles apply to another form of vocal prayer to which it seems many are called today, and which can also be a way in to contemplative silence.

Many Christian people, though they probably will not speak of it unless it be to one or two like-minded friends, use some sort of vocal prayer frequently repeated such as the Jesus Prayer, which was made known to the Western world largely through *The Way of a Pilgrim*, first published in English about fifty years ago. Perhaps this book is the best introduction to the prayer, for we there meet it kindled in a human heart.* Its full form is, 'Lord Jesus Christ, Son of the Living God, have mercy on me a sinner.' But it has various shorter forms and can be reduced to the oft-repeated single word, 'Jesus'. It is not of course just an exercise of the lips. Far from it! The heart and mind will be, in a very simple and unstrained way, enfolded in what is being said.

I should only want to commend this prayer to those who have a special drawing to it. But I think some form of repetitive vocal prayer (with cautions against indiscriminate use which we shall come to later), is likely to be a help to many who have not yet found the Jesus Prayer. The psalms, of course, supply an inexhaustible treasury: 'Praise the Lord O my soul, and all that is within me praise his holy name'; 'Make me a clean heart O God, and renew a right spirit within me'; 'Be still and know that I am God.' Equally, we could take something much longer, such as a psalm known by heart, or a collect, or verses of a hymn. Whatever it is thus becomes to us *our* office, and like the offices of the Church not only does it preserve us from a dissipation of our energies (recall those three parallel lines), but it is a launching pad for the silent prayer of the heart. It has to be used with discretion and there can be a danger of a zeal which outruns wisdom. It is always good if we can turn to some experienced person with whom we can discuss these things. In using such prayers what is important is to mean 'God', and to go on meaning God—whether the actual words at any particular moment seem to have meaning for us or not. When the words fade away into the background, we can still mean God beyond the words.

Here we return to the question of vain repetition. Let me put it

*For another excellent description of this way see the chapter, 'The Prayer of the Name' in *Prayer* by Abhishiktananda (SPCK), a French Benedictine monk who made his home in India. See also *The Power of the Name* by Kallistos Ware (SLG Press) which is probably the finest short exposition of this prayer written in the last few years (1974, revised edition 1977).

another way. Hammering can be vain repetition if the nail moves not a fraction of an inch, but if each blow takes it, even minutely, nearer its destination, the hammering is no longer vain. So too, if every repetition of prayer helps to unite us, however little, more closely with God who is the end of all prayer, the repetition is not vain but profitable. It is right to go gently with this form of prayer, keeping it within our means and using it for perhaps not more than ten minutes at a time at first; we can then see how we are taken on from there.

The Jesus Prayer is particularly associated with the Eastern Orthodox tradition, and it is therefore in the classical collection of spiritual writings known as the *Philokalia* that we should look for advice concerning its use. And here we find stress laid, not once but a number of times, on what is called 'bringing the mind into the heart'—a phrase that applies equally well to the Jesus Prayer and to various other forms of words. We are helped to learn this by looking mentally towards the heart and, as we do so, we find after a time that for short periods the prayer becomes, as it were, lodged in the heart and will go on for a while of its own accord. In a beautiful little book on *The Invocation of the Name of Jesus* (published by the Fellowship of St Alban and St Sergius) a lovely likeness is drawn between this form of prayer and the flight of a bird, it may be that of an eagle. Through the measured beating of her wings the great bird ascends steadily higher and higher into the upper reaches of the air. Then for a time the wings are spread and still as she glides in graceful flight. Presently, when height has been lost, the motion of the wings begins again. So with our prayer, whatever form it takes, the actual repetition of the words will ebb and flow and yet, for those practised in it, the prayer itself will be ever carried in the heart. What matters in life beyond all else is that the mind and heart of man be stayed on God—whether we call this habitual recollection, prayer without ceasing, or something else—and only insofar as it serves that end is repetitive prayer to be cherished and practised.

A note of warning is needed here, however, because this form of prayer, used indiscriminately, can stir the unconscious levels of the mind beyond our immediate capacity to deal with them. It has been powerfully and cogently said that 'the pain of deepening self-knowledge is to be kept not at a bearable minimum, nor at an intolerable maximum,

C

29

but at a creative optimum'. Interpret that packed sentence in relation to food and then transfer it to the realm of prayer. In eating, there is a creative optimum, the amount which best suits us for our daily work. Below that there is a bearable minimum, but this leaves us too weak adequately to meet life's demands. And above it is an intolerable maximum which over-taxes the digestion and provides the body with more than it can assimilate. So too, at every stage, there is a right proportion in prayer. However, with that caution, let it be said that the need is more generally to stimulate and encourage the timid than to restrain the over-confident. Some of my readers will have known this way of prayer for a long while; to others it may be new. I would suggest to these latter: if your heart warms to this way of prayer and you feel a desire to embark on it, then in all probability the Holy Spirit is leading you to test it for a while. But if what has been said makes no appeal, then equally you may be fairly sure that this is not your way, at least for the present—and, indeed, many people are taken on into silent contemplation without experiencing this type of vocal prayer as a stage in their spiritual life.

Yet we are still only on the threshold of our subject. What I have been describing is perhaps best seen as a 'way in' to contemplative prayer. Often it forms a sort of passage from one type of prayer of which we do not hear very much today though it was widely practised in the past—the prayer of meditation. We shall not spend long on this but it is worth saying a few words. As Christians use the word (Eastern religions use it in a different sense), meditation means, basically, taking some passage, usually from the Bible, reading it, pondering over it, considering what bearing it has upon one's own life and one's relationships with others, and forming some resolution pertaining to the theme; at the end there will be free prayer of some kind. The Bible Reading Fellowship offers one of the many schemes available to those whose prayer is along these lines. It is thus that many of us have been launched on our prayer life and if we find such a pattern fruitful we should continue to follow it. Let me add that the way of contemplation does not mean there is no longer a place for the meditative hearing and reading of scripture and other books relating to the faith. What it does mean is that we shall find these occupations now do no more than touch the fringe of what we might call our real prayer.

For there comes a time in the lives of many people when this way of meditation is no longer satisfying. Even more, it becomes very difficult, indeed practically impossible, for them to follow it in their times of prayer. If this development is accompanied by a deep longing for God, if we find ourselves just wanting him and him alone, then we may take this as an indication that the Holy Spirit is leading us on into contemplative prayer, and we must be content to leave discursive meditation behind and yield to the prompting of the Spirit. 'Like as the hart desireth the water brooks, so longeth my soul after thee, O God.' 'When I awake after thy likeness I shall be satisfied.' Aspirations such as these, whether constant or recurring, may be taken as sure signs of the call to contemplation. At the same time, everyday things will very probably become less satisfying than before and there may be some withdrawal on our part, but in the end we are likely to come back to all the good things of God's creation, though now in a different way—now they will be caught up in the love of God and in the overflow of our prayer into the whole of daily life.

★　　★　　★　　★　　★　　★

What I am describing is, of course, a well-trodden path on the pilgrimage of the spirit. St John of the Cross is a reliable authority here and three times in his writings he points to the signs of this development. Many readers will recognise it as a stage in their own life, perhaps experienced many years ago. But, just as when you are motoring without a map and find yourself in unfamiliar country, you think anxiously that you may have lost the way, so some people for whom their former ways of prayer are no longer possible, become worried and discouraged, and because the silent ways in which they are now being led involve so much simplification of memory and mind and will, they may begin to ask whether they are praying at all. Very possibly they now try to turn back to the old way and, finding it fruitless, are tempted to give up altogether. This is where knowledge of the well-tried paths of the spirit can reinforce our faith and enable us to persevere. What is happening has been neatly summarised by Father Stanton in a short definition by which he distinguishes meditation from contemplation: 'Meditation is a detachment from the things of the world in order to attend to the things of God. Contemplation is a detachment from the things of God in order to attend to God himself.'

Before we go further we ought to make it clear that this silence of which we are speaking is not the silence of blankness or idleness, which has nothing to do with the drawing of the Holy Spirit. There are two images we might use to describe it. Think of a sentry on duty, an image of silence as alertness or awareness; or think of two people who love one another deeply, an image of silence as understanding and perception and harmony. We all know how different silences can be. There can be an idle silence or an embarrassed silence—better than either of these is conversation, in which we try to develop an awareness of one another's needs and interests. But that is only a stage (just as discursive meditation is only a stage), and sooner or later there will be a break-through and long periods can then pass, perhaps before the fire of a winter's evening, when each is supported by the silent presence of the other and conversation is superfluous or, rather, both are free to let it come or go at will. That is the picture of contemplative silence.

In approaching contemplative prayer in this way, I do not want to imply that people nowadays are generally drawn to contemplation through the earlier discipline of meditation. Historically speaking this is no doubt true, but formal meditation is much less taught and practised today and the contemplative call is likely to be a direct one. Anyone who finds within his heart an answering cry to St Augustine's great words, 'Thou hast made us for thyself and the heart of man is restless till it finds rest in thee', and who is ready in the grace of God to face the testing experiences of that quest should go forward, nothing doubting, on the path to which the Spirit is now calling him.

CHAPTER VI

Contemplation and the Cloud of Unknowing

IN PURSUIT of our study of contemplation we will now turn to a book which has very much come into its own in our day, the fourteenth-century *Cloud of Unknowing*. It is available in various editions both medieval and modern, but for practical purposes I would recommend the Penguin version in present-day English. In a valuable introduction the translator, Clifton Wolters, describes the anonymous author as a man of 'well-stored and scholarly mind, with a flair for expressing complexities simply,' and he goes on to say: 'There was more than a streak of the poet in him, and at the same time a saving sense of humour and proportion. Probably most people will feel that they would like to know him, and some at least might wish they could have his guidance today.' This is what I propose we now seek.

The *Cloud* was written to a young disciple who had, it seems, appealed to the author for training in prayer. Through him it is addressed to a larger public, and yet by no means to everybody nor even to every devout Christian, but only to those who, by the inner working of the Spirit, God has disposed towards contemplation. We have already considered what constitutes that disposition.

Chapter Three begins, 'Lift up your heart to God with humble love and mean God and not what you get out of him.' Here at the very start we are reminded of a suggestion I made earlier that we should try to see prayer as an offering. Now part of that offering must be the offering of time, and about this we must be clear from the outset. It is almost too obvious to need saying that if there is to be prayer there must be time set apart for prayer. I am not suggesting that this is easy in an ordinary household, but I believe it would have to be an extraordinary household for it to be impossible. But once the time is set aside and adhered to, the battle is more than half won. The fact is that prayer is so much like hard work that most of us find that very ordinary things like writing a letter or making a telephone call take on an exaggerated importance when the time for prayer comes round. But to continue: 'Hate to think of anything but God himself, so that nothing occupies your mind or will but only God. Try to forget all created things . . . let them go, pay no attention to them . . . Do not give up but work away . . . When you first begin you find only darkness and a cloud of unknowing . . . Reconcile yourself to wait in this darkness as long as necessary, but go on longing after him you love . . . '; and again, 'strike that thick cloud of unknowing with the sharp dart of longing love and on no account think of giving up.'

Let us make a brief pause here. We have taken up our position for prayer, we have called upon the Holy Spirit, vocally or in the silent language of the heart, and we are now to let everything go, our thoughts, our imaginations, our memories, everything except this one thing that remains—and here is a phrase which keeps recurring in *The Cloud*—'a naked intention towards God and him alone'. The one thing necessary, we are told, is to 'mean God who created you and bought you and graciously called you to this state of life.

But how can we retain this intention in practice? We shall almost certainly need some simple thought as a focal point for the mind, and so the author allows us a word such as 'God', or 'love', or some other word given to us. This word he says is to be 'fixed fast to the heart' (and here we are reminded of the teaching in the *Philokalia* about 'bringing the mind into the heart') so that, our author continues, 'it is always there, come what may. It will be your shield in peace and war alike.' There is no need for the word to be framed with the lips, unless it is a help to do so, whether aloud or under the breath. The time will come when we can, as it were, mentally see the word where it lodges in the heart, and that is best of all.

But we should not feel bound to any word. A word is given for our help if we need it. The author writes (ch. 39), 'if God leads you to certain words, my advice is not to let them go, that is, if you are using words at all in your prayer.' Ultimately they will tend to slip away, and we shall be left simply looking into the heart and meaning God, and continuing to mean him and him alone. What the author insists on in regard to words, if they are used, is that they should be taken whole and not analysed. If, for example, we take the word 'God', we should resist the temptation to reflect on him, for this is not the time to consider discursively his love and goodness, nor his reconciling work in our Lord's passion. There is a time for that but it is not now; now is the time for knowing God and loving him, the time—inevitably we come back to the phrase—for 'reaching out with a naked intent of the will towards God', remembering always that, mentally, we should be looking into the heart and seeing him there.

The Cloud does not say much about posture. The author simply tells us that the body will of its own accord tend to take up the position most suited to prayer. In Chapter Sixty-one he writes,

> For when a soul is determined to engage in this work, then, at the same time, (and the contemplative does not notice it) his body, which perhaps before he began tended to stoop because this was easier, now through the Spirit holds itself upright, and follows physically what has been done spiritually. All very fitting!

Whether kneeling, sitting or standing, the back invariably tends to straighten out in this prayer, as all who practice it will know. We shall be returning to this question, but I would just mention here that older people, and perhaps many younger people too, may well find that sitting erect in an upright chair is the best position. There are some to whom sitting suggests a want of reverence, but we need hardly feel like that about a posture that our author may quite possibly have used himself. We know that it was the favourite posture of one of the great English mystics of the period of *The Cloud*. To quote from Father Verrier Elwyn's book *Richard Rolle*:

> 'Sitting', he would say, 'I am most at rest and my heart most upward. I have loved to sit, for thus I loved God more and I remained longer within the comfort of love than if I were walking or standing or kneeling.'

And we may recall that it was while the Church was seated that the Holy Spirit first descended upon it at Pentecost.

Described thus, prayer sounds easy enough, and indeed in Chapter

Three of *The Cloud* the author does make the claim that it is the easiest work of all, when a soul is helped by grace and has a conscious longing for prayer. No doubt there is a real sense in which that is true. We may recall the story of Jacob in the Old Testament, how he toiled seven years for Laban, in order to win Rachel's hand. From what we know of Laban, Jacob's work must have involved a good deal of sweat and tears, and yet, we are told, for the love that he bore to Rachel they seemed to him but a few days. It was love that made the work easy, and that is true also of our work of prayer. At the same time, the author is at no pains to conceal the cost involved. 'It is hard work', he writes, 'very hard work indeed' (ch. 26).

It is probably no accident that he refers to his prayer as work for prayer has about it two qualities which we normally associate also with work. On the one hand it is costly to the one who does it, and on the other, beneficial to the community, which includes the worker himself. If we are called to contemplative prayer and mean to respond to that call, we must face the fact that this will require a great deal of us—the sacrifice of time, courage to persevere, patience to endure the pain of deepening self-knowledge, fortitude in times of temptation, faith when the way is obscure, and the love which is ready to make every new surrender as the Spirit calls. That is one side of the work, the costly side, and we may well ask who is sufficient for these things? But there is too the other side, the social side which serves the community, and how can we serve the community better than by engaging in the work of healing and reconciliation, of making men whole within the Body of Christ? For that is the effective outcome of this work. It has been well said that contemplatives war against the real enemy, and ultimately against the only enemy, for whereas in the world we are up against effects, the contemplative is brought face to face with causes, with the ultimate truths which lie behind the visible.

★　★　★　★　★　★

Some of my readers will remember a story by Robert Hugh Benson in which he tells of a lonely chapel where a nun is praying. To this chapel comes one whom we might call a visionary or a sensitive, someone who possesses unusually perceptive psychic sensibility. To the ordinary observer nothing is happening in that chapel— there is simply a nun praying—but to the visionary the unseen world discloses its secrets. Teilhard de Chardin re-tells the story:

> All at once he [the visionary] sees the whole world bound up and moving and organising itself around this out-of-the-way spot, in tune with the intensity and inflection of that puny, praying figure. The convent chapel becomes the axis about which the earth revolves. The contemplative sensitised and animated all things because she believed; and her faith was operative because her very pure soul placed her near to God.

'This piece of fiction', Teilhard adds, 'is an admirable parable', and he continues:

> If we could see the light invisible as we can see the clouds or lightning or rays of the sun, a pure soul would seem as active in this world by virtue of its sheer purity, as the snowy summits whose impassable peaks breathe in continually for us the roving power of the high atmosphere.

The author of *The Cloud* does not hesitate to make this sort of claim for his work on what we might call the community side. He writes thus:

> All saints and angels rejoice over it and hasten to help it on with all their might . . . Moreover the whole of mankind is wonderfully helped by what you are doing in ways you do not understand. Yes, the very souls in purgatory find their pain eased by virtue of your work . . . and in no better way can you be made clean or virtuous than by attending to this.

How little we know of our true helpers! Father Martin Thornton observes in *Christian Proficiency*:

> I rather feel that some of us are in for a shock when in the Church expectant we discover the real perspective for world redemption; the achievement of the Prime Minister and the Foreign Secretary may look pretty small compared with the influence wrought by little Miss Perkins of Honeysuckle Cottage.

And do we realise that as we grow older and the vigour of mind and body begin to decline, this is the work which the Holy Spirit desires to entrust increasingly to the faithful, the work which the author of *The Cloud* does not hesitate to describe as the most far-reaching and deepest work of all?

CHAPTER VII

Contemplation and the Cloud of Forgetting

OUR AUTHOR tells us us there are two clouds, not one, and it is to the second, the 'cloud of forgetting' that we must now turn our attention. We meet it first in Chapter Five where he writes as follows:

> Just as this cloud of unknowing is as it were above you, between you and God, so you must also put a cloud of forgetting between you and all creation . . . Everything must be hidden under this cloud of forgetting . . . Indeed, if we may say so reverently, when we are engaged on this work it profits little or nothing to think even of God's kindness or worth, or of our Lady, or of the saints or angels, or of the joys of heaven . . . it may be good sometimes to think particularly about God's kindness and worth . . . yet in the work before us it must be put down and covered with the cloud of forgetting.

The author allows no exception. He goes on to specify everything that must be put under this cloud. We have already seen that any theological speculation is forbidden at this time; equally forbidden are all memories and imaginations of happy occasions and beautiful things, all the anxious thoughts and painful memories which may so often, even against our will, rise up and trouble us—memories of past sins long since repented and forgiven—all these are to be pressed down, like everything else, under the cloud of forgetting. This is not for the destruction of memory and imagination—at other times they will function in the ordinary way—but in and through the practice of this prayer they will be increasingly purified and we ourselves will grow in detachment from them. The near compulsive grip which memory and imagination may have upon us in certain areas of our lives will be broken, and as we give ourselves to this prayer the Spirit will lead us on into an ever growing freedom.

As the book goes on the author becomes yet more insistent on this cloud of forgetting. What is likely to cause special trouble, he says, is the memory of past sins, yet we are to be in no way disheartened by this. Here, in its entirety, is Chapter Thirty-one:

> When you have done all you can to make the proper amendment laid down by Holy Church, then get to work quick sharp. If memories of your past actions keep coming between you and God, or any new thought or sinful impulse, you are resolutely to step over them, because of your deep love for God; you must trample them down under foot. Try to cover them with the thick cloud of forgetting as though they had never been committed by you or anyone else. And indeed as often as they come up push them down. And if it is really hard work you can use every dodge, scheme and spiritual strategem you can find to put them away. These arts are better learnt from God by experience than from any human teacher.

Is there something alarming in the vigour of these words? Do they perhaps suggest 'repression' in the psychological usage of the word? By repression I do not mean the same thing as *suppression* of thought—something which occurs every time we choose to think of one thing rather than another as, for instance, when the bell goes, a schoolboy will suppress the thought of Latin in order to free his mind for mathematics. Repression as I am now using the word stands for a compulsory and involuntary forgetting of experience or memories which the mind has found too painful to retain in conscious thought. A mark of real repression is that the memory cannot be recalled at will, however hard the person may try. That does not mean it is out of harm's way—this is certainly no case of 'out of sight out of mind'—for it can send up all sorts of fears and compulsions to the conscious mind, and many people suffer physical disability—sickness, paralysis, blindness—through fears and conflicts which remain repressed. When I read somewhere, 'You mean, doctor, I have a boil in my unconscious?', it seemed to me a nicely graphic description of a repression. Psychologically speaking, *suppression* is harmless, *repression* is dangerous. It is convenient to have the two words, standing as they do for different concepts, and yet they cannot be kept entirely apart, for suppression could be followed by repression, if the former were persistent and the thought suppressed highly charged with emotion.

From what the author of *The Cloud* writes in the next chapter (Thirty-two) which we shall come to later, I think he would have been fully alert to the danger of repression, psychologically understood. The great spiritual directors were good psychologists, though since they lived in a bygone age their knowledge of the science was necessarily intuitive rather than analytical. I have been interested to read in Dr Morton Kelsey's book, *Healing and Christianity*, how he, the author, asked Jung what was the method of counselling nearest to Jung's own. He expected Jung to name one or other of the psychological schools, but instead he replied, 'The classical direction of conscience of the nineteenth century in France'. The directors of that period would have drawn freely on those before them; names such as St Francis de Sales, Fénelon, Caussade and others come to mind.

★　★　★　★　★　★

Before we go further, let us distinguish between different types of memories. First there are what I shall call the emotionally neutral class, and these are by far the most numerous. What is it I have done today? Well, if I think back, I got out of bed, I washed and dressed, had breakfast, walked to work, and so on. All such memories belong to the emotionally neutral class, and if they recur during prayer they are not difficult to ignore and should cause no trouble. Then there are other thoughts which may be emotionally evocative, but in a pleasant and non-disturbing way. Such are the memories of beautiful scenery, great art or music, friendship and the like. These too are to be put down at the time of contemplative prayer, and it is unlikely that any problem will arise. More difficult to put away is the memory of some work in which the mind has been deeply engrossed, some business problem, some talk one is preparing, some difficult letter to be written.

However, in none of these cases is there a danger of repression in the sense in which we are using the word. But there are other thoughts which, for one reason or another, will fit into none of these classes, thoughts which are highly charged emotionally, due to some painful or traumatic experience, forgotten or largely forgotten, reaching back, perhaps, into early childhood; or to some persistent and it may be irrational fear which takes on the strength of a phobia we are virtually powerless to control. Morbid guilt, overwhelming grief, deep-seated resentment, wounded pride, jealousy, a sense of inferiority, scrupu-losity, more or less compulsive aggressions—these are the kind of disorders, disguised as they may be in consciousness, which are likely to cause trouble. But we must take courage, for in our prayer they are finding their healing.

The author, as we have seen, has said that everything is to be pressed down under a cloud of forgetting, but, significantly, he immediately goes on to say how memories can be dealt with when they do arise, and here, as everywhere else, he is clearly speaking from his own expe-rience. Let me clarify this seeming contradiction by a simple illustration.

Suppose you take your ten year-old son to church and, since he has a tiresome cough, you tell him not to cough during the sermon. At once you realise that this piece of advice standing alone will not do, yet it has value because it gives him something to aim at—without it he might cough freely and unnecessarily. 'But', you go on to say, 'if you must cough, try to cough into your handkerchief and then the noise will be muffled.' It is a very simple illustration but that is the sort of advice our author is giving. He is telling us not to let memories and imaginations invade our prayer, and this is valuable because it sets our sights on God alone, and on the word we have chosen to focus and hold our attention. Without that advice we should be lost from the start. However much this boy of ours may have to cough in church, it is essential he should get his priorities right and aim at self-control. If he doesn't he will spoil the sermon for everyone else and would have done better to stay at home. Equally, if we do not get our priorities right in prayer, if we do not firmly resolve 'to reach out with a naked intent of will towards God' so that mind and heart are occupied with nothing else but God himself, then we shall find ourselves given over to the memories and distractions which crowd in and our prayer time will be a disaster—daydreaming rather than praying—and it would have been better not to attempt it. But once our sights have been truly set on God, with the desire and intention that in God's grace they shall remain so, we need not fear these invaders of our imagination. What now becomes necessary is to pay them no attention. Later I hope to show that these very things are the means of our purification and healing, so long as we are content simply to let them be, and look over their shoulder, as it were, to God.

CHAPTER VIII

Contemplation and Healing

'LOOKING over their shoulder, as it were, to God'. With these words we have, in fact, anticipated the teaching of *The Cloud*; in Chapter Thirty-two we read:

> Do everything you can to act as if you did not know that these thoughts were strongly pushing in between you and God. Try to look over their shoulder seeking something else—which is God, shrouded in the cloud of unknowing.

We are then to keep looking towards God, to be ready to suffer distractions if need be, 'to let them float', in the language of popular psychology, but not to attend to them. We are neither to run away from them nor to encourage them, we are simply to look to God in the midst of them.

The word 'simply' is not meant to imply that this will be easy. It is not for nothing that the author calls prayer 'hard work', and there will be days when the going is tough. I am not suggesting a sinecure for retirement and old age! Rather, what I am describing will call for quite as much resolution in the realm of the spirit as climbing a mountain in that of the body—the work is for men, not for canaries. Here is a quotation from John Edward Southall, a Quaker of several generations ago, which describes an early experience of silence before God. A friend had suggested he should learn to be still in God's presence. This, he thought, would be an easy matter—but not at all. No sooner had he begun

> than a perfect pandemonium of voices reached my ears, a thousand clamouring notes from without and within, until I could hear nothing but their noise and din. Never before did there seem so many things to be done, to be said, to be thought, and in every direction I was pushed and pulled and greeted with noisy acclamations of unspeakable unrest. It seemed necessary for me to listen to some of them, but God said 'Be still and know that I am God'. As I listened and slowly learnt to obey and shut my ears to every sound, I found after a while that when the other voices ceased, or I ceased to hear them, there was a still small voice in the depths of my being that began to speak with an inexpressible tenderness, power and comfort.

This was an early venture into silence, made at a time when no doubt the writer's daily life was marked by all sorts of distracting and dissipating thoughts, and we may believe that as the spirit of recollection formed within him, this disturbance at the time of prayer tended to abate. But we must not over-simplify, for there will be disturbances in prayer whose origin is other than that of our lower consciousness. The gospels and the epistles both remind us of the forces of evil beyond ourselves. St Paul tells us that we fight not against flesh and blood, but against principalities and powers, against spiritual wickedness in high places. At such times too we may draw on fields of psychic force set up by other people far and near. Jung's postulate of a collective unconscious is suggestive here. However this may be, our own rule remains the same—to look to God, to mean God and to go on meaning God. In standing firm within the storm, accepting its batterings, yet looking beyond it to God himself, the end for which we and all men have been created, we are being used by the Spirit to neutralise and disinfect evil whatever its origin—and, more, to work for its transformation. This is the prayer-ward aspect of what St Paul says (Col. 1:24) about completing 'what is lacking in Christ's afflictions, for the sake of his body, that is the Church'.

We notice that John Edward Southall did not have just a single word such as 'God', or 'love', with which to focus his attention, but a complete phrase, 'Be still and know that I am God'. The author of *The Cloud* also commends this. In Chapter Seven he gives us this tenderly beautiful phrase in the power of which distraction may be overcome, 'Him I covet, Him I seek, and none but Him'. No doubt he would say here, as he has said of the single word, that we should take whatever sentence God gives us—from the Psalms, it may be.

Our author tells us that when the conflict is at its height, the image of looking over the shoulder to God, who is beyond, may need to be changed for another better suited to the challenge of prayer. We are, he says, to surrender ourselves to God in the hands of our enemies, and he bids us pay special heed to this suggestion 'for I think that if you try it out it will dissolve every opposition'. The picture might be that of a manacled prisoner, quite helpless and at the mercy of his conqueror, and all that is left for him to do is to give himself over utterly and completely into God's care. 'Why art thou so vexed, O my soul, and why art thou so disquieted within me?' When such words come spontaneously to our lips, that is the moment for complete surrender—not to our state or to our despondency—but to God in the midst of our state. That also was the psalmist's experience. 'O put thy trust in God, for I will yet give him thanks which is the help of my countenance and my God'.

★ ★ ★ ★ ★ ★

For an exposition of this trustful surrender, or 'abandonment' as it is more generally called, let us turn now to the classical spiritual writer on the subject, Père de Caussade, confessor and director in the eighteenth century to the Sisters of the Visitation in France. It will be good to draw briefly on his letters to these Sisters through which the theme of abandonment runs like a golden thread. To one of them he writes that when troublesome thoughts cannot be expelled from the mind—in this case he is speaking of excessive fears—'no other remedy remains but to bear this crucifixion in a spirit of total self-abandonment to the will of God'; and this is saying precisely what *The Cloud* is saying—'surrender yourself to God in the hands of your enemies'. We have of course at such times the perception—of faith, not of feeling, for 'clouds and darkness are round about us'—that God is holding on to us, never more perhaps than now. Imagine a cat holding her kitten in her mouth and making her way through the undergrowth. The journey may be a painful one for the kitten, leading through thorns and briars, but the small creature knows she is being held. That picture illustrates the passive side of the spiritual life; it needs to be balanced at other times by the active side and for that we need the picture of a baby monkey, who is not held, but clings for dear life to its mother as she makes great leaps from tree to tree. Just so is the Christian life a matter of holding on, until we are led into the knowledge that we are being held.

In all his many letters to the Sisters, Caussade never shows the least alarm at the afflictions they are called upon to bear. To another he writes, 'I will end this letter by telling you that your state is truly crucifying and for that reason sound, desirable, purifying and sanctifying.' He has already told her that the interior fever which seems to destroy her is indeed only destroying the impure and earthly elements, much as various poisons in the body are destroyed during the crisis of illness. This, he adds, is a sign of recovery, not of sickness. And of course he is right. Caussade is not talking here of the healing of the body but of the soul, or, if we prefer, the total healing of the whole man, and in modern language we should say, that in this standing in the storm, in patient endurance, with faith unbroken, the personality is being integrated, the disharmonies of our nature are being resolved into a single whole, we are being taken on by the Spirit to a fuller maturity in Christ, which in its turn makes possible a deeper relationship in love.

Naturally, this healing process is not restricted to the time of prayer. What is begun or comes into special prominence in our prayer life will be carried forward in all our occupations. For the man whose life is

D

immersed in the love and will of God in prayer, the healing will continue through the whole round of life—his work and recreation, his eating, drinking and sleeping, his family relationships, his service of others and their service of him. Further, we must see this healing process not just as something taking place within ourselves—the healing of all men is in some degree caught up in it. We cannot separate ourselves as though we were all little islands set here and there in a universal sea. We need an organic picture, such as St Paul gives us of the body, in which the healthy functioning of each part has its effect for good on the body as a whole.

Here then is our liberation, and in its measure it contains within it the liberation of all. I think of those undying words on the tombstone of Martin Luther King, 'Free at last, free at last, thank God Almighty, I am free at last!' Man longs for his full liberation, for liberation and the capacity for love go forward hand in hand. The opposite of liberty is bondage, and bondage means fear, and it is, as St John tells us, perfect love that casts out fear. That is to say, perfect love liberates, and we may therefore say that liberation makes possible the perfection of love. For purposes known only to God our liberation may often be delayed, finding its perfection only after passing through the gate of death and resurrection. We can only place ourselves in the hands of the Spirit, content to be taken on at his pace, believing that God's purposes are best served in ourselves, and through us in those around us, when we let him refashion us in his time and not in ours. Meanwhile our infirmities and oddities, our annoyances and quirks remain, serving not only to humble us, but perhaps to present the sort of challenge to those around us which each needs from the other, until at last we are brought, in St Paul's undying words, to 'the glorious liberty which belongs to the children of God'.

CHAPTER IX

Some Practical Points

TOGETHER we have studied *The Cloud* or, at least, what lies at the heart of its teaching, and we have learnt in some measure how we are to proceed in the prayer of contemplation, and how to deal with the memories and imaginations which threaten to defeat us. Let us now imagine that we are coming to the time of prayer.

But, first of all, why are we coming? Surely, because we believe in a general way that this is the kind of prayer to which the Holy Spirit is calling us. We have already discerned the signs of that call and we need not now refer to them again. But we are also coming because this *is*, for us, the time for prayer, the occasion of our self-offering. We are not coming because we feel like praying—perhaps we do, more probably we do not—and it may even be that praying is the last thing in the world we feel like doing. It is essential that we get this clear. To be ruled by feeling, by sense impression, is a mark of spiritual immaturity. The mature are ruled by faith. Every act of prayer is an act of faith. Father de Caussade wrote in *Abandonment to Divine Providence*, 'Faith is nothing else than a continual pursuit of God through everything that disguises, misrepresents, and so to speak annihilates him.' Is that not exactly what our feelings, our sense impressions—whether gathered from external events or from our internal vagaries—are continually doing? If Job, in that great drama of the Old Testament, deprived of his possessions, bereaved of his children, and afflicted with suffering, had relied on what he saw and heard and felt, he would have taken his wife's advice, cursed God and died. Only the eye of faith could penetrate the cloud of affliction experienced in the senses and affections and cry out, 'Though he slay me, yet will I trust him'. So too, when feelings are against us, whether before or during prayer, it is only by acts of faith that we can reject them for the frauds they are, and pursue our appointed way.

Nor need we complain because this is so—we ought rather to rejoice, for every temptation to deny prayer on account of feeling carries within it the opportunity to grow in faith. Archbishop Temple once said that if we prayed for patience, we must expect God to answer our prayer by giving us opportunities in which to exercise it. The same principle is true if we pray for faith or, for that matter, for any grace. This time of prayer is the moment when faith is nourished and quickened, and never more so than when mood and feeling are against us. Faith has been defined by C. S. Lewis as the activity of holding on to what reason has accepted, in spite of changing moods. It is, he says, telling mood and emotion where they get off when they threaten to carry out a blitz on the reason.

In the life of the spirit there has to be a stripping of the senses which involves throwing the whole burden on to faith, not because the senses are evil—no one who believes in the Incarnation can accept that—but because they are so supremely good that neither God nor man can be satisfied with anything less than the realisation of their full potential. And that can come about only through a cleansing process—the pruning of the vine that it may bear more fruit—a vital part of which takes place in the prayer that is informed by faith at those times when the senses are being deprived of what they are most wanting. As St John of the Cross tells us, man has to be led from the stage at which his will rests and feeds on sense experience, to one in which the joys of sense are not, ultimately, denied but known in liberty of spirit. That is the true joy for which we were created, and the experiences of aridity and the 'dark night' in prayer are a preparation for it, both by what the Spirit effects within us at the time and also by the creation (in the power of the same Spirit) of those dispositions which will enable us to meet the disciplines of life in such a way that he can use them to complete his work in us.

★　　★　　★　　★　　★　　★

Yet there will undoubtedly be days when we shall need the support of a book to help us through the difficult seasons of prayer. We are like children learning to walk, and we need a rail to hold on to and to come back to after each unaided trial. It is better frankly to acknowledge and accept this need than to persevere in a way which may, for the present, be too hard for us.

Spiritual reading, as it is generally called, differs from discursive meditation in that the mind and imagination are now channelled very simply by the words or sentences before us. We do not think around our subject but accept each passage as it comes and allow it to 'dissolve in the mind as a sweet dissolves in the mouth'. The simile is Caussade's and could scarcely be bettered, as long as we remember that what the mind feeds on is always to descend to the heart. We read the passage slowly, extracting the flavour of each sentence before allowing ourselves to go on to the next. The successive pauses may last for a minute, or much longer, and even if whole periods of prayer sometimes pass in this way it need be no cause for worry. But as soon as we find that reading is coming in the way of a deeper silence, the book should be laid aside, at least for the time being. Until then our reading will give mind and imagination just as much material as they need on which to feed. This is no different in principle from the one word 'fixed firmly in the heart', or the single sentence recommended in *The Cloud*. Spiritual reading is performing the same function, but at an earlier stage, allowing the mind and imagination more diversity than can be supplied by the single word or sentence.

The passage needs to be chosen with care; anything which stimulates intellectual excitement or curiosity is worse than useless, and for that reason readings that are well-known are likely to be the most suitable— we shall not be so eager to see how the theme ends when we know already. We should let the Holy Spirit lead us to the books which will best minister to our varying needs. Psalms, hymns and some books of prayer lend themselves specially to being read sentence by sentence, with frequent pauses. Letters by masters of the spiritual life such as St Francis de Sales, Caussade, Fénelon and others allow for longer readings between each break, and the same is true of many spiritual classics, the *Confessions* of St Augustine, *The Imitation of Christ*, as well as other works both ancient and modern.

★   ★   ★   ★   ★   ★

Then, a second question in respect of our approach to prayer: how long are we here for? We shall certainly not get far unless we do fix a definite time—even if in practice it may often have to be cut short. How this is done will of course depend on circumstances, and those of a single person living alone will be very different from those of a busy housewife. But let us not overlook the possibility of keeping the prayer time in church where we shall be relatively free from noise and disturbance. Group meetings too, whether in church or elsewhere, can be a great help; we support one another in the silence, are encouraged to be regular, and the temptation to cut the time short is eliminated. Today the Holy Spirit seems to be calling many people in this way.

Then, thirdly, in what state have we come? Are we perhaps tense and keyed up? Certainly we do not come to prayer in order to be relaxed (though prayer will have this effect on us), but if we are tense it is doubtful if we shall ever have the resolution to begin. We need a 'phasing-in' period. In the East yoga is commonly used for this; taking up various postures helps to release tensions and lead the disciple into the stillness of meditation. Some people are now discovering this in the West (though I do not refer here to the schools of yoga which use it simply as a bodily discipline cut off from its spiritual roots). But there are other ways of phasing-in and we probably know how to find our own. For some people it will be gardening, for others knitting, weaving, music, going for a walk. What is common to all these activities, if they are wisely chosen, is that they help to relax body and mind.

Vocal prayer of the sort described earlier can also, of course, be a 'way in'— so can a very simple act of relaxation. Indeed to spend the first few minutes at the start of prayer in this way may often be the best way to begin. We hear a good deal about relaxation nowadays, and bearing in mind its close relationship with prayer, it will be worth saying a few words about it here.

First, what is *not* meant by relaxation is lazing away one's time in idleness. As a working definition I would suggest that a relaxed state is a state of creative awareness attained 'through the lessening and elimination of mis-directed tension and effort'. The quotation is from a brochure by Ursula Fleming, a teacher of relaxation (though I prefer to call her art 'creative relaxation') who goes on to describe it as a 'way of growth both in the life of prayer and into a fuller humanity'. The dictionary defines the word primarily in terms of loosening, slackening, reducing tension, but that is too negative for our purpose and whenever I use the word in the present context it should be taken to include also the positive idea of creative awareness.

Suppose we approach the subject from the point of view of human relationships. Have you ever said to yourself, 'I do enjoy spending an evening with X, I always come home so refreshed and relaxed'? Yet you did not visit X in order to become relaxed, but to get to know him better and take pleasure in his company and conversation—that you came away relaxed was a by-product of the event. And does it not, by analogy, ring true that if in our prayer we are really in touch with the creative love and being of God, we should emerge fresh and relaxed? But the illustration does not end there. On occasion you might equally have to say, 'My time with X yesterday was quite different from before—I was so tense when I arrived that I was unable to absorb what he was waiting to give me.' And you may well decide that the next time you visit him you will relax beforehand so as to be able to reap the full benefit of his company. Surely this too applies to prayer. We may be so tense before we begin that we can no more establish rapport with the Holy Spirit, nor he with us, than we could really meet our friend on that unfortunate evening. So if we feel tense before prayer, it makes sense to begin by relaxing in order to become more receptive to what the Spirit would give us. Prayer is not relaxation and relaxation is not prayer, but for the Christian a vital partnership exists between the two, and if, in the way of the Spirit's leading, you say that you are now going to relax for the love of God, you are proposing to do something at least as close to prayer as when you say you are going to garden for the love of God, or knit for the love of God. As we have already noted, all these and many similar occupations, by providing relaxation for mind and body, can help to lead us into true prayer.

Relaxation does not mean 'going all of a flop'—it does not mean doing nothing. It certainly may look to others as if you were doing nothing and you may on occasion think the same thing yourself. I sometimes say to people who think they are doing nothing in their prayer, Well, just for once, stop praying and *really* do nothing—make yourself a cup of tea, sink back into an arm-chair, let the mind go where it will. You will see how easy it is, and that will show you how hard you must have been working before. The same could be said about relaxation—even after a person has accepted the idea of it, the practice of relaxation will call for the same courage and resolution as the practice of prayer itself.

Yet we should proceed cautiously, and before we leave the subject it ought perhaps to be said that relaxation is not (as popular articles sometimes suggest) in itself a magic cure for all our troubles. The truth is that relaxation *per se* is neither good nor bad but morally neutral. In this respect it may be compared with sleep which has the same function of enabling us to perform our work more effectively, quite independent of any moral value attached to the activity of sleeping. Yet I suspect that relaxation (and sleep too), taken in its proper measure, has a built-in tendency towards goodness. However this may be, everything I am saying here is based on the presupposition that we are seeking a fuller knowledge of God and of his will and purpose in our lives—that is the context of our reflections. We are considering relaxation in relation to prayer, and prayer in relation to living. And we might remind ourselves that the kind of prayer we have been speaking of is allowed by the author of *The Cloud of Unknowing* only to those who are seeking to grow into the fullness of Christ and who believe they are being called to follow this way of contemplation.

★   ★   ★   ★   ★   ★

Finally, we return to the question of posture in prayer. We pray as whole persons, not as disembodied spirits, nor yet as spirits inside a body as water is inside a bottle, but as a complex entity of body, soul and spirit. To neglect the role of the body would be to deny that side of our nature of which we are, generally speaking, most conscious. As we have already seen, if we want to go to sleep the sensible thing to do is to take up the posture best suited to sleep, and if we want to pray to take up the posture the body finds most natural for prayer. Like the author of *The Cloud* we may have already discovered that posture for ourselves.

SOME PRACTICAL POINTS

The basic requirement in posture is that the back should be held straight in an easy tension. This applies in whatever position we adopt—whether we stand, sit or kneel upright; or kneel sitting on the heels, perhaps with the help of a cushion or a prayer stool. Sitting on the floor lotus fashion with legs crossed and feet tucked into the body is an inadvisable posture for most western people, unless they have trained themselves to hold it easily. The rule should be to adopt whatever position we can maintain without undue strain. Let us assume we have chosen to sit on an upright chair. Holding the back straight in an easy tension will assist a natural counter-relaxation of the temples and forehead, and the muscles of the face and jaw. The mouth should be shut, but not tightly so. The eyes will be closed, eyeballs down and relaxed, and we look mentally to the heart. The arms too will be relaxed, the hands resting relaxedly palms downwards on the upper part of the thighs, or palms upwards in the lap. The classic position for the head is erect, firmly set on the neck, the back, neck and head forming one straight line. Some find that when the head is slightly inclined forward it assists in looking mentally at the heart. You will notice how often we come back to the traditional Orthodox teaching of 'the mind in the heart'.

I believe there is value in knowing and saying these things but I would not wish to be over-assertive about them—I have great respect for the approach of *The Cloud*, which is to lay down no rules but simply allow the body to straighten out naturally to its correct position as the prayer proceeds. Yet I am sure there is need for this other approach as well and it must be left to the individual to find the right balance between the two.

Of course we are not going to imagine, that having adopted the most meticulously correct posture, we are now at prayer. All we have done is try to prepare for the Spirit to do his work in us. I have described only the dry bones of the valley, which the Spirit must breathe on and clothe with flesh if they are to live. Or again, we are like the servants at the wedding feast who were told to fill the water-pots with water. Only the Lord of life can turn it into wine.

CHAPTER X

The Practice of Contemplation

WE NOW COME to the prayer itself. Picture, if you will, three concentric circles. On the circumference of the outer circle are written the names of the five senses—*sight, hearing, touch, taste, smell.* Also written there are the words *imagination* and *memory*; and lastly, on the same circle, *intellect* and *will.* The space outside the circle represents the world of everyday affairs, and these nine faculties inscribed on the circumference are to be understood in their normal relationships to all the things which go on happening around us. As the Spirit enables us to pray we leave this outer circle behind and move to the circumference of the middle circle. And with us we shall take *memory* and *imagination* and also *intellect* and *will,* but not the five senses. These are left behind and so should be mentally erased from the outer circle, but only lightly, because we shall come back to them. It is easiest to understand what is meant by saying we leave the five senses behind if we think of it in relation to sight. In prayer we close the eyes and so shut out the visual sense altogether. We cannot in the same direct physical way shut out the other senses. For example, if a car passes on the road, we cannot escape hearing it, but as far as possible we pay it no attention.

Here we are then on the middle circle, and now we have to deal with memory and imagination. We can think of these as one, for memory is really part of imagination. When the imagination is aware of something which happened to us in the past we call it memory. When we simply imagine something outside our own experience, then that is pure imagination and memory plays no part. Only imagination, moreover, can have reference to the future. St John of the Cross likens these two faculties to a sixth sense, and it is not difficult to see why. I may close my eyes and shut out all that is visible, but I can still, in my imagination, 'see' my car in the parking place outside. There is even an English phrase for

54

it, 'seeing with the mind's eye', which exactly expresses St John of the Cross's meaning. In the same way, if you are musical you can probably 'hear with the mind's ear', playing back to yourself through the imagination some favourite concerto. The same is true of all the senses and you will see at once where this line of thought is taking us. If it makes sense in prayer to close the eyes and cut out *seeing*, then it makes no sense at all to retain the faculty of 'seeing with the mind's eye'— that is to say, using imagination to recapture the sense of sight. It is pointless to bolt the doors of the senses against the thief and at the same time leave the windows of imagination and memory open. Either we leave the house open or we close it altogether. It will be clear that this argument applies equally to all the senses in their relation to memory and imagination.

My object in stressing this point is to reinforce the teaching of *The Cloud*. There, you will remember, we are told not only to look at the cloud of unknowing before us, but to put a cloud of forgetting beneath us. Memories and imaginations are to be resolutely stepped over or, to use another metaphor, we are to look over their shoulder to God who is beyond. And having just seen that memory and imagination are as it were a sixth sense— windows through which the thief may get into the house after we have locked all five doors—we are in a position to see why the teaching of *The Cloud* must be as it is, and could not indeed be otherwise. And that is a point gained, for while everyone accepts that it is quite reasonable to cut oneself off from sight, and as far as possible from noise and other distractions of sense during prayer, when it comes to the question of leaving behind memory and imagination as well, they ask whether perhaps this is not taking things a little too far. But we have seen that if we allow entry to these two faculties we might just as well allow it to the five senses, and that will be disastrous for our prayer.

But now we move in from this middle circle to the inmost circle, lightly erasing, for the time being, memory and imagination to which we shall return later. To the circumference of the third circle we bring *intellect* and *will*. 'Intellect' is now to be understood not in its discursive form but as the ability to know by intuition rather than reasoning, and 'will' is to be understood as the ability to love by a single act and not by a multiplicity of acts, as we normally do in everyday life.

★   ★   ★   ★   ★   ★

Here then the Holy Spirit has brought us to the heart of our prayer. In the language of *The Cloud* we are to lift up our hearts to God, with humble love to mean nothing but God, to try to forget all created things, to strike the thick black cloud of unknowing with the sharp dart of longing love, and on no account to think of giving up. The short word 'fixed firmly in the heart' as the focal point of our attention is to be 'our shield and spear'.

Yet we know only too well that memory and imagination, although left behind, will be continually trying to force their way in and divert our attention from this work of prayer. What are we to do then, when despite our desire to give our attention exclusively to God, we perceive these things trying to gain a foothold within us? Certainly there is nothing to be afraid of. If the will remains constant they can do us no harm or, more positively, they can become the means of strengthening the will in its resolution to mean God and him alone.

Here is a picture I have found helpful. Imagine you are taking a motor launch up a river and your eye is on the goal you want to reach—in this context, God himself. Coming downstream and floating by is all sorts of rubbish—bits of wood from broken-up packing cases, empty tins and bottles and soggy paper thrown overboard by picnic parties, flotsam and jetsam of every kind. All this represents the memories and distracting thoughts which float across the mind and seek admission during prayer. What are we to do with them? We are to let them float past us. *Floating*, as you probably know, is a word frequently used in practical psychology—let your anxieties float, we are told—and all this rubbish is to float. That does not mean we are to try not to see it. Even if we do so try it will not help; a part of the mind will inevitably be aware of it. The important thing is not to follow it, that is to say, not to occupy ourselves with examining the thoughts or fears or fancies which may at any moment present themselves. We are to let them come, see them briefly, and let them go. Zen Buddhism has a picture of distracting thoughts being like empty boats floating down a river, and bids

56

us watch those boats but resist the temptation to jump on board.

Our position then with regard to this rubbish is that we neither encourage it nor do we run away from it. We notice it briefly and, without pausing to examine it, we pass on our way through it. It is in this experience of standing and looking to God that our healing is taking place. We have already seen in the last chapter that we cannot separate our own healing from that of others, that all mankind is in a measure caught up in what God is doing in us. And so this work of standing in the conflict is most truly a work of intercession, a work of reconciliation between God and all men, of whom I am one.

The world and the devil may have their part in this rubbish which is floating by, but much of it will be of the flesh—my flesh—using the word to stand for the whole lower nature: pride, anger, jealousy, along with avarice, gluttony lust and sloth. Memories float by, the unconscious may throw up material that the conscious mind had repressed and which now appears in disguise, just as dreams disguise the lower levels of the mind. Here is the carcase of a cat floating towards us—a pretty smelly piece of garbage this, and we shall get a whiff of it as it goes by—but never mind, it won't kill us. We have only to remain constant, looking to God our saviour and redeemer, as Peter, walking across the stormy water, looked to Jesus. It was only, we remember, when he ceased to look at Jesus that he began to sink. There will indeed be suffering in all this but it will be creative—the suffering of purgation and cleansing. The place where the Spirit is bringing our disintegrated personalities into unity and harmony is the place of healing. We may not know it at the time, but later we shall be able to say with Jacob, 'Surely the Lord is in this place and I knew it not'.

Illustrations tend to break down at one point or another and there is a weakness in the one we have chosen. We have said that we are to take our boat upstream with eyes fixed on the goal before us, which is God. This however gives us an image of 'God out there' which is not helpful for our purpose, when we have already stressed the importance of keeping the eyes of the mind directed towards the heart. So the limitations of our example must not mislead us here. You might also object that, so far, it suggests that only painful, disagreeable and worthless things will occupy the imagination during prayer, whereas we know this is by no means true. Not only rubbish, but swans and water-lilies, trees and clouds reflected in the stream will glide past our boat—in other words, memories of what is good and pleasing will also seek to claim our attention. Our rule here is as before. We may see but we may not examine. The point is that *all* considerations are as dross for our purpose at this time. To examine some memories selectively, 'when they are holy and promise well', would be to make us prisoners whose liberty is equally curtailed whether the rope that binds us is of silk or rough hemp.

Father de Caussade has another picture which may help us at such times. He says we are simply to allow these memories and distractions to drop away as one might let stones drop into the sea. We are to resist them by turning to God with renewed acts of trust and abandonment. We are ever to keep plunging ourselves afresh into the ocean of God's love. Fénelon calls this forgetting of self the most perfect penitence, 'because all conversion consists only in renouncing self to be engrossed in God'.

But we are not to be worried if our distractions do not drop away as we might wish. Sometimes these stones which are to fall into the sea appear to be more like rubber balls which float around us. What matters is that the attitude of our will should be like an open hand, ready to let go. The very act of opening the hand helps us to let go with the mind. We may encourage ourselves with an old Chinese proverb, 'You cannot prevent birds flying round your head, but you can prevent them making nests in your hair.'

★　　★　　★　　★　　★　　★

And now our prayer time is over. What is it we have been doing? Well, in a sense, we have been taking a holiday, and if that sounds an odd way of putting it, remember that holidays often include doing hard and challenging things, like climbing mountains, or exploring unknown country. But this has been the best sort of holiday, for not only have we 'got away from it all'—which is essential on any holiday—but we have been in touch with the fount of all life and so have found *re-creation* of mind, body and spirit. We know how important it is to get

58

away from our work from time to time, not to neglect it, but in order to see it in the perspective of eternity. And so we return to our work as before, and yet, not quite as before, for in this prayer the Holy Spirit has been active in the depths of our being, cleansing and purging us, healing and unifying the various sides of our nature. As a result we bring to our work a deeper integrity, a clearer perception of the real needs of those around us and—having come to grips with these things within ourselves—a fuller understanding of the fears and tensions which threaten to overwhelm others. Above all we bring a love disciplined and made strong through an ever deeper union with God himself.

EPILOGUE

'Love is my meaning'. These words, adapted from Mother Julian, hold the key to all that has been said and all that can still be said, whatever the nature of our calling in prayer. No method of prayer can of itself be valid apart from the dimension of love. In prayer love is expressed and deepened, and yet more, it is re-fashioned as, in an ever renewed dying and rising again, it takes its form from the wisdom and perfection of God. The saints are the great lovers, but it is God's love which is shed abroad in their hearts, and no other than God's redeeming and saving love will avail. 'At eventide they will examine you in love.' So wrote St John of the Cross, and the quotation is commonly ended there. We need to reflect that he at once went on to say that it is not the human love of our natural temperament of which he speaks, but the love which partakes of the nature of God's own love. And this he describes elsewhere as a living flame which tenderly wounds the soul at its deepest centre. What a corrective is this to our own poor human notions, often more sentimental than strong, more possessive than pure, more spoiling than wise, more tolerant than true! How well would St John of the Cross have understood—and we too shall grow to understand—the saying which an early tradition attributed to Jesus, 'He that is near me is near the fire'!

THE POSITIVE ROLE OF DISTRACTION

IN PRAYER

ROBERT LLEWELYN

'HE PRAYS BEST who does not know he is praying.' This well-known saying of St Antony of Egypt does not refer—certainly need not refer—to any 'advanced' level of prayer. It can be paralleled in almost every activity. We must all have had the experience, for example, of a train journey with an engaging companion, or it may be an absorbing book, when the miles have sped by and for long periods we have been unaware that we were travelling. So in prayer it is likely that there have been times when we have become so caught up in what we were doing that we have lost the very thought of our doing it. It is only as we were emerging from this deeper experience of prayer that we became truly aware of it at all.

It may often be far from clear what has happened at such times. Sometimes it may seem that there has been just a blank, though for how long this has lasted we may have little idea. We recall that when we began our prayer we placed ourselves in the hands of the Holy Spirit, and it is reasonable to think that in the blank of this 'lost' period we have for a few minutes been held in that stillness which is God. Certainly that would make sense of the deep draught of refreshment and peace we have found.

INVOLUNTARY DISTRACTION

Yet sometimes as we look back on such moments we know that at least as we were emerging from them our minds were fastened on some definite subject. It could have been something quite trivial, or it might have been a more weighty matter such as the remembrance of a friend in need, or perhaps some personal question such as a difficult decision to be made. Whatever it was, we had not intended that our attention should rest here; our desire when we went to prayer was to turn to God and him alone. We have, in technical language, experienced an involuntary distraction, that is to say (by definition) a distraction in which the will plays no part. Naturally there is no blame attached to a happening of this sort. The temptation now, however, may be to follow up and search into the subject of our distraction, or deliberately to allow the mind to continue to engage on it. To obey this impulse would be to make the distraction voluntary, for it is only at this point that personal choice and responsibility enters in. The movement from involuntary to voluntary distraction is avoided if, as soon as we become aware that the mind is resting on something other than God, we take up our prayer again in the manner in which it was begun, looking to God and him alone.

THE MANNER OF OUR PRAYING

We shall return to this point later and enquire its meaning, but first let us ask of what sort of prayer we are speaking, and the manner in which we are to engage in it. I am speaking of simple contemplative prayer such as I have sought to describe elsewhere[1] along the lines of what is now a widely read fourteenth century work, *The Cloud of Unknowing*. The marks of the calling to that prayer are discussed in the prologue and last chapter of the *Cloud*, and in many books, generally based on the classical exposition to be found in the writings of St John of the Cross.[2] To one or other of these the reader must be referred. Here it is only possible to recapitulate briefly the manner of the prayer. The following sentences from the *Cloud* do not necessarily appear consecutively in that work. They are taken together for convenience, the better to draw out the heart of its teaching.

Lift up your heart to God with humble love; and mean God and not what you get out of him. Hate to think of anything but God himself so that nothing occupies your mind or will but only God. Try to forget all created things. Let them go and pay no attention to them. Do not give up but work away. When you begin you find only darkness and a cloud of unknowing. Reconcile yourself to wait in this darkness as long as is necessary, but go on longing after him you love. Strike that thick cloud of unknowing with the sharp dart of longing love, and on no account think of giving up. You are to reach out with a naked intention directed towards God and him alone. Mean God who created you, and bought you, and graciously called you to this state of life. Let some such word as 'God' or 'love' or some other word given to you, be fixed to your heart so that it is always there come what may. It will be your shield and spear in peace and war alike. If God leads you to certain words my advice is not to let them go, that is, if you are using words at all in your prayer. Should any thought arise and obtrude itself in the darkness, asking what you are seeking, and what you are wanting, answer that it is God you want: 'Him I covet, him I seek, and him alone.'

Just as this cloud of unknowing is, as it were, above you and between you and God, so you must put a cloud of forgetting between you and all creation. Everything must be hidden under this cloud of forgetting. Indeed, if we may say so reverently, when we are engaged on this work it profits little or nothing to think even of God's kindness or worth, or of our Lady, or of the saints and angels, or of the joys of heaven. It may be good sometimes to think particularly about God's kindness and worth, yet in the work before us it must be put down and covered with the cloud of forgetting.

When you have done all you can to make the proper amendment laid down by Holy Church then get to work quick sharp. If memories of your past actions keep coming between you and God, or any new thought or sinful impulse, you are resolutely to step over them because of your deep love for God. Try to cover them with the thick cloud of forgetting. And if it is really hard work you can use every dodge, scheme, and spiritual stratagem you can find to put them away. Do everything you can to act as if you did not know that these thoughts were strongly pushing in between you and God. Try to look over their shoulders seeking something else which is God shrouded in the cloud of unknowing.[3]

Here, then, we are at the beginning of our prayer time, looking to God as the Spirit enables us, meaning God, holding to a word (it may be) to focus our attention, and it could well be that the whole time or prayer is spent in this way. But it will not always be so. A period may intervene when the word to which we are holding (or it may be our *consciousness* of a naked intent towards God) has disappeared, and we are left either in blankness, or in what we have described earlier as involuntary distraction. The point to note is that it is only as we are emerging from this period that we recognize it for what it is. If we now find that our mind has been engaged on something other than God we are not to be concerned about that, or to think that our prayer has gone wrong. On the contrary we should accept this as the Holy Spirit's work. However, now that this period of what we may rightly call transcended consciousness is over, we again take up our word, or proceed in whatever manner we were engaged when we began our prayer. To do otherwise would be, as explained earlier, to turn an involuntary distraction into a voluntary one, and this is always weakening to prayer.

INVOLUNTARY DISTRACTION A POINT OF HEALING

Involuntary distraction, however, far from being weakening is in fact a healing point. At whatever stage we are we stand in need of healing, both for our own sakes and for the sake of the whole Body of Christ. In St Paul's words, 'If one member suffers, all suffer together; if one member is honoured all rejoice together.' (I Cor. 12:26.) We all stand in need of wholeness, the completion of the work of the Holy Spirit bringing our discordant personalities into a unity of being in Christ. Prayer is a time when this work is being taken forward; as it is also a time when we are prepared to be receptive and open to the Spirit as he meets us in the experiences of everyday life. When the Holy Spirit takes us during prayer to an involuntary distraction we may take it that this is a focal point for growth towards wholeness. Often it will be that the point on which the mind comes to rest is holding a pocket of tension which needs to be released, and this moment of prayer is for the discharging of it. More specifically, such moments might be for the dispelling of a fear, the resolving of a doubt, the healing of a memory, the weakening of a prejudice, the scattering of a vanity, the deepening of a relationship. It may help to see the Spirit as an all-wise psychotherapist who takes his patient now to one point, now to another, in the movement towards integration and wholeness.[4] Sometimes we can see clearly why this or that is chosen, but at other times we must be content to wait in darkness, and trust his better wisdom. There is no need for us to know. It may often be that the mental image is camouflaging, as in a dream, the real point where healing is taking place. All that is necessary is that we are assured that this is a healing point, for we can then approach involuntary distractions in a positive way, instead of seeing them as spoiling our prayer, or worse still receiving them with feelings of guilt as though we have here an indication that we have not properly fulfilled our part. Our need, rather, is to reflect that in this experience ground has been gained, rather than that there has been a falling back into defeat.

PRAYER AND SLEEP

We have said earlier that prayer not only takes forward the healing process, but prepares us to be receptive to the operation of the Holy Spirit through all the occasions of life. I want to consider one such area which is perhaps given far too little attention generally by Christian people. Sleep in its proper measure is one of God's greatest gifts to man. Many know this by experience; others are less fortunate and know it largely by deprivation. 'He giveth his beloved sleep' runs the familiar text of the psalms, though probably more accurately rendered in modern versions in some such phrase as 'he gives *to* his beloved *in* sleep'. The well-loved Compline words 'I will lay me down in peace and take my rest', point to the way in which we may best receive God's gifts in sleep. They presuppose a life of dedication, a life in which prayer is a regular and living feature. The prayer of surrender, of relaxation into the arms of God is the best of all preparations for sleep.

Apart from being the great restorer of physical and mental energy, sleep brings us healing through nature's mechanism of the dream. Clinical tests in our time have revealed the importance of dreams as a contributory factor to mental health, and it is well known that one of the unfavourable effects of barbiturate-induced sleep is that normal dreaming is suppressed. Professor J. A. Hadfield says of dreams that they are a part of the drive of the psyche towards wholeness, and speaks of them as 'releasing repressed experiences and emotions . . . striving to restore the personality to efficient functioning as a whole. However distressing many of the dreams may be they are always working for our health'.[5] Putting ourselves under God's protection as we go to sleep, must we not believe that the Spirit once again takes us to those points which need his liberating touch? The work begun in prayer opens the way for the Spirit's further healing in sleep.

Dreams normally do their work independently of our capacity to interpret them. Were it to be otherwise nature would surely have presented us with a mechanism by which we might remember them. Unpleasant and frightening dreams tend to disappear as we move on in the Christian life, and this is partly so because prayer itself releases tensions and repressed emotions which would otherwise need to find their discharge in sleep.

What about sleep in prayer? If, as sometimes happens, sleep overtakes us, it can be deeply refreshing, and should no more worry us than an involuntary distraction. It can be just about impossible to pray when we are tired, and I should prefer to be more positive and say that a brief sleep can be—like a period of deliberate relaxation before prayer—an excellent preparation for the remainder of the prayer time. We need not hesitate to see it as God given, bringing needed refreshment to mind and body. What is referred to here is sleep in the physiological sense, and is not to be confused with those times of prayer of which later no account can be given, to which my opening quotation from St Antony refers.

FURTHER THOUGHTS ON INVOLUNTARY DISTRACTION

What we have described earlier is a true involuntary distraction. Yet it may not be at all what we usually mean when we use that term. I fancy we generally think of involuntary distraction as taking place at the primary level of prayer when the will is too weak to hold on. But how difficult, if not impossible, to tell where that point lies! Like the driver of the car who goes to sleep at the wheel, we shall always suppose that a little more resolution was within our power. There are too many imponderables in prayer for any reliable judgement to be made, and I do not suppose we should attempt to make one. It is enough that we shall allow such occasions to be a reminder of our poverty apart from God's enabling strength, and it may well be that this awareness is our deepest need. We should, however, remember that it is not the straying of the attention which destroys prayer. Only the withdrawal of the *intention* can do that.

It may be too that this is the moment for the changing of the imagery during prayer. Our quotation from the *Cloud* speaks of trying to look over the shoulder of distracting thoughts seeking God who is beyond. Another picture the author advises is that of surrendering to God in the hands of our enemies 'for I think that if you try it out it will dissolve every opposition'.[6] Note that the surrender is to God, not to the distracting thoughts. Father de Caussade is one of the great exponents of this deeply suffering—and also, as he explains, purifying, cleansing, healing—side of prayer.[7]

VOLUNTARY DISTRACTION

So much then for involuntary distractions. How about those which are voluntary? We have seen from our quotation from the *Cloud*, and we shall certainly know it from our experience, that no sooner have we set ourselves to prayer than all sorts of unbidden memories and imaginations are likely to arise. It is the intentional diverting of the mind from God, to attend to these clamorous voices which constitutes a voluntary distraction. By definition there can be no such distraction without (to a greater or lesser degree) the consent of the will. Clearly, voluntary distraction is of necessity weakening to prayer. It must, however, be sharply distinguished from the temptation to it, which in common with all temptation that is neither sought nor encouraged, can become the means through which the resolve of the will is strengthened. It is therefore not distraction itself, but the challenge offered by the temptation it presents, which has in this case a positive role to play.

What are we to do in the presence of these voices which cry out for our attention? The *Cloud* says we are to look over their shoulder seeking God who is beyond. As we have seen, this is the first of the two pictures the author gives to assist us in the work of prayer. Even so it does not lie in our power to be unaware of them. We can ignore them, we can disregard them (these are both words which belong to the will), but a state of unawareness (a word which belongs to the imagination) is not open to us. They have to be allowed to 'float', rather as rubbish floats by a river launch, our own attention at the helm being on the goal we desire to reach.

I once read the story of a fisherman who having to be away at sea for many weeks used to preserve his catch in tanks that it might be fresh on his return. Even so, these fish never quite had the flavour of those which were freshly caught, at least not until he hit upon the idea of adding catfish to the tanks. Not all his fish can have lived, but those which did were said to taste the better for having to be vigilant to the end against their natural foe. No need for us to put catfish in the tank! They will be there already, waiting to flex the spiritual muscles of those who survive.

CONCLUDING THOUGHTS

Descriptions intended to clarify sometimes do more to confuse. There is the fable of the centipede who after working out for his puzzled brother the order in which to marshall his legs, found he was never able to walk again. It can be rather like that in prayer. In the end only the Holy Spirit can be our teacher, and rules must always be giving place to his beckoning and our response. At one time we are the rower pulling laboriously at the oars, at another the sailor carried before the breeze. Yet the oarsman draws his strength from God, and the boat under sail needs human skills to direct it. In the last analysis it will be the prayer which the Holy Spirit gives us which will be the 'best', whether seen as being for God's glory or as the meeting of our need for deliverance: twin aspects of prayer which must always be held together. 'For their sakes I sanctify myself'—the words of Jesus which take us to the heart of prayer stand in a passage saturated with adoration of the Father. St Irenaeus has the thought we are looking for: 'The glory of God is a living man; and the life of man consists in beholding God.'

NOTES

1. See *Prayer and Contemplation*, Fairacres Publication 46, SLG Press. This article follows on from everything written in that pamphlet and ideally, I like to think, should be read in conjunction with it.

2. See *Ascent of Mount Carmel*, Book II, chapter XIII.

3. *The Cloud of Unknowing*, translated into modern English by Clifton Wolters, Penguin Classics, 1961.

4. A correspondent—an analytical psychologist—writing in *The Times* of 12.4.75 on forces from the unconscious which have the power to heal or destroy, says, 'It is only through an integration of these unconscious images that the fragmentary alienated ego-consciousness becomes a psychic whole. The more man is split off from the other side, i.e. unconscious, the more he is liable to outbursts of affect and obsessions.' Prayer takes forward this healing process, and I believe this to be especially true of the prayer here under consideration.

5. J. A. Hadfield, *Dreams and Nightmares*, Pelican.

6. Op. cit., chapter 32.

7. See *Abandonment to the Divine Providence*. The current paperback edition does not, however, include the letters to Sisters which best convey Caussade's teaching. *Prayer and Contemplation* (referred to in n.1) deals with this in chapter 3.

THE POWER OF THE NAME:

THE JESUS PRAYER IN ORTHODOX SPIRITUALITY

by
Archimandrite
KALLISTOS WARE

My doctor is Jesus Christ, my food is Jesus Christ, and my fuel is Jesus Christ. — Contemporary Coptic Monk

Prayer and silence

'When you pray,' it has been wisely said by an Orthodox writer in Finland, 'you yourself must be silent. . . . You yourself must be silent; let the prayer speak.'[1] To achieve silence: this is of all things the hardest and the most decisive in the art of prayer. Silence is not merely negative—a pause between words, a temporary cessation of speech—but, properly understood, it is highly positive: an attitude of attentive alertness, of vigilance, and above all of *listening*. The hesychast, the man who has attained *hesychia*, inward stillness or silence, is *par excellence* the one who listens. He listens to the voice of prayer in his own heart, and he understands that this voice is not his own but that of Another speaking within him.

The relationship between praying and keeping silent will become clearer if we consider four short definitions. The first is from *The Concise Oxford Dictionary*, which describes prayer as '. . . solemn request to God . . . formula used in praying'. Prayer is here envisaged as something expressed in words, and more specifically as an act of asking God to confer some benefit. We are still on the level of external rather than inner prayer. Few of us can rest satisfied with such a definition.

Our second definition, from a Russian *starets* of the last century, is far less exterior. In prayer, says Bishop Theophan the Recluse (1815-94), 'the principal thing is to stand before God with the mind in the heart, and to go on standing before Him unceasingly day and night, until the end of life.'[2] Praying, defined in this way, is no longer merely to ask for things, and can indeed exist without the employment of any words at all. It is not so much a momentary activity as a continuous state. To pray is to *stand before God*, to enter into an immediate and personal relationship with Him; it is to know at every level of our being, from the instinctive to the intellectual, from the sub- to the supra-conscious, that we are in God and He is in us. To affirm and deepen our personal relationships with other human beings, it is not necessary to be continually presenting requests or using words; the better we come to know and love one another, the less need there is to express our mutual attitude verbally. It is the same in our personal relationship with God.

1 Tito Colliander, *The Way of the Ascetics* (London 1960), p. 79.
2 Cited in Igumen Chariton of Valamo, *The Art of Prayer: An Orthodox Anthology*, translated by E. Kadloubovsky and E.M. Palmer (London 1966), p. 63.

In these first two definitions, stress is laid primarily on what is done by man rather than God. But in the personal relationship of prayer, it is the divine partner and not the human who takes the initiative and whose action is fundamental. This is brought out in our third definition, taken from St. Gregory of Sinai (†1346). In an elaborate passage, where he loads one epithet upon another in his effort to describe the true reality of inner prayer, he ends suddenly with unexpected simplicity: 'Why speak at length? Prayer is God, who works all things in all men.'[1] *Prayer is God*—it is not something which I initiate but in which I share; it is not primarily something which *I* do but which *God* is doing in me: in St. Paul's phrase, 'not I, but Christ in me' (Gal. 2:20). The path of inner prayer is exactly indicated in St. John the Baptist's words about the Messiah: 'He must increase, but I must decrease' (John 3:30). It is in this sense that to pray is to be silent. 'You yourself must be silent; let the prayer speak'—more precisely, let God speak. True inner prayer is to stop talking and to listen to the wordless voice of God within our heart; it is to cease doing things on our own, and to enter into the action of God. At the beginning of the Byzantine Liturgy, when the preliminary preparations are completed and all is now ready for the start of the Eucharist itself, the deacon approaches the priest and says: 'It is time for the Lord to act.'[2] Such exactly is the attitude of the worshipper not only at the Eucharistic Liturgy but in all prayer, public or private.

Our fourth definition, taken once more from St. Gregory of Sinai, indicates more definitely the character of this action of the Lord within us. 'Prayer', he says, 'is the manifestation of Baptism.'[3] The action of the Lord is not, of course, limited solely to the baptized; God is present and at work within all men, by virtue of the fact that each is created according to His divine image and likeness. But this image has been obscured and clouded over, although not totally obliterated, by man's fall

---

1 *Chapters*, 113 (PG 150, 1280A). See Kallistos Ware, 'The Jesus Prayer in St. Gregory of Sinai', *Eastern Churches Review* iv (1972), p. 8.

2 A quotation from Psalm 118 [119]:126. In some English versions of the Liturgy this is translated, 'It is time to do [sacrifice] unto the Lord', but the alternative rendering which we have used is richer in meaning and is preferred by many Orthodox commentators.
The original Greek uses the word *kairos*: 'It is the *kairos* for the Lord to act'. *Kairos* bears here the special meaning of the decisive moment, the moment of opportunity: he who prays seizes the *kairos*. This is a point to which we shall return.

3 *Chapters*, 113 (PG 150, 1277D).

into sin. It is restored to its primal beauty and splendour through the sacrament of Baptism, whereby Christ and the Holy Spirit come to dwell in what the Fathers call 'the innermost and secret chamber of our heart'. For the overwhelming majority, however, Baptism is something received in infancy, of which they have no conscious memory. Although the baptismal Christ and the indwelling Paraclete never cease for one moment to work within us, save on rare occasions most of us remain virtually unaware of this inward presence and activity. True prayer, then, signifies the rediscovery and 'manifestation' of this baptismal grace. To pray is to pass from the state where grace is present in our hearts secretly and unconsciously, to the point of full inward perception and conscious awareness when we experience and *feel* the activity of the Spirit directly and immediately. In the words of St. Kallistos and St. Ignatios Xanthopoulos (fourteenth century), 'The aim of the Christian life is to return to the perfect grace of the Holy and Life-giving Spirit, which was conferred upon us at the beginning in divine Baptism.'[1]

'In my beginning is my end.' The purpose of prayer can be summarized in the phrase, 'Become what you are'. Become, consciously and actively, what you already are potentially and secretly, by virtue of your creation according to the divine image and your re-creation in Baptism. Become what you are: more exactly, return into yourself; discover Him who is yours already; listen to Him who never ceases to speak within you; possess Him who even now possesses you. Such is God's message to anyone who wants to pray: 'You would not seek Me unless you had already found Me.'

But how are we to begin? How can we learn to stop talking and to start listening? Instead of simply speaking to God, how can we make our own the prayer in which God speaks to us? How shall we pass from prayer expressed in words to prayer of silence, from 'strenuous' to 'self-acting' prayer (to use Bishop Theophan's terminology), from 'my' prayer to the prayer of *Christ in me*?

One way to embark on this journey inwards is through the Invocation of the Name.

'Lord Jesus . . .'

It is not, of course, the only way.

No authentic relationship between persons can exist without mutual

---

1 *Century*, 4 (PG 147, 637D). The idea of prayer as the discovery of God's indwelling presence can be expounded equally in terms of the Eucharist.

freedom and spontaneity, and this is true in particular of inner prayer. There are no fixed and unvarying rules, necessarily imposed upon all who seek to pray; and equally there is no mechanical technique, whether physical or mental, which can compel God to manifest His presence. His grace is conferred always as a free gift, and cannot be gained automatically by any method or technique. The encounter between God and man in the kingdom of the heart is therefore marked by an inexhaustible variety of patterns. There are spiritual masters in the Orthodox Church who say little or nothing about the Jesus Prayer.[1] But, even if it enjoys no exclusive monopoly in the field of inner prayer, the Jesus Prayer has become for innumerable Eastern Christians over the centuries the standard path, the royal highway. And not for Eastern Christians only:[2] in the meeting between Orthodoxy and the West which has occurred over the past sixty years, probably no element in the Orthodox heritage has aroused such intense interest as the Jesus Prayer, and no single book has exercised a wider appeal than *The Way of a Pilgrim*. This enigmatic work, virtually unknown in pre-revolutionary Russia, has had a startling success in the non-Orthodox world and since the 1920s has appeared in a wide range of languages.[3] Readers of J.D. Salinger will recall the impact of this 'small pea-green cloth-bound book' on Franny.

Wherein, we ask, lies the distinctive appeal and effectiveness of the Jesus Prayer? Perhaps in four things above all: first, in its simplicity and flexibility; secondly, in its completeness; thirdly, in the power of the Name; and fourthly, in the spiritual discipline of persistent repetition. Let us take these points in order.

---

1 The Jesus Prayer is nowhere mentioned, for example, in the authentic writings of St. Symeon the New Theologian or in the vast spiritual anthology of Evergetinos (both of the eleventh century).

2 There existed, of course, a warm devotion to the Holy Name of Jesus in the medieval West, and not least in England. While this displays certain points of difference from the Byzantine tradition of the Jesus Prayer, there are also obvious parallels. The present paper makes no attempt to discuss the western Invocation of the Name; this must be the theme of some future essay. For a brief treatment of the subject, see John A. Goodall, 'The Invocation of the Name of Jesus in the English XIVth Century Spiritual Writers', *Chrysostom*, vol. iii, no. 2 (1972), pp. 113–17.

3 It has even been translated recently into one of the major languages of the Indian sub-continent, Mahratti. The introduction to this translation has been written by a Hindu university professor who is a specialist in the spirituality of the Name: see E.R. Hambye, SJ, in *Eastern Churches Review* v (1973), p. 77.

Simplicity and flexibility

The Invocation of the Name is a prayer of utmost simplicity, accessible to every Christian, but it leads at the same time to the deepest mysteries of contemplation. Anyone proposing to say the Jesus Prayer for lengthy periods of time each day—and, still more, anyone intending to use the breathing control and other physical exercises in conjunction with the Prayer—undoubtedly stands in need of a *starets*, of an experienced spiritual guide. Such guides are extremely rare in our day. But those who have no personal contact with a *starets* may still practise the Prayer without any fear, so long as they do so only for limited periods—initially, for no more than ten or fifteen minutes at a time—and so long as they make no attempt to interfere with the natural rhythms of the body.

No specialized knowledge or training is required before commencing the Jesus Prayer. To the beginner it is sufficient to say: Simply begin. 'In order to walk one must take a first step; in order to swim one must throw oneself into the water. It is the same with the Invocation of the Name. Begin to pronounce it with adoration and love. Cling to it. Repeat it. Do not think that you are invoking the Name; think only of Jesus Himself. Say His Name slowly, softly and quietly.'[1]

The outward form of the prayer is easily learnt. Basically it consists of the words 'Lord Jesus Christ, Son of God, have mercy on me'. There is, however, no strict uniformity. The verbal formula can be shortened: we can say 'Lord Jesus Christ, have mercy on me', or 'Lord Jesus', or even 'Jesus' alone, although this last is less common. Alternatively, the form of words may be expanded by adding 'a sinner' at the end, thus underlining the penitential aspect. Sometimes an invocation of the Mother of God or the saints is inserted. The one essential and unvarying element is the inclusion of the divine Name 'Jesus'. Each is free to discover through personal experience the particular form of words which answers most closely to his needs. The precise formula employed can of course be varied from time to time, so long as this is not done too often: for, as St. Gregory of Sinai warns, 'Trees which are repeatedly transplanted do not grow roots'.[2]

---

1 'A monk of the Eastern Church', *On the Invocation of the Name of Jesus* (The Fellowship of St. Alban and St. Sergius, London 1950), pp. 5-6. (Reprinted by SLG Press, 1970, pp. 2-3.)

2 *On stillness and the two ways of prayer*, 2 (PG 150, 1316B).

There is a similar flexibility as regards the outward circumstances in which the Prayer is recited. Two ways of using the Prayer can be distinguished, the 'free' and the 'formal'. By the 'free' use is meant the recitation of the Prayer as we are engaged in our usual activities throughout the day. It may be said, once or many times, in the scattered moments which otherwise would be spiritually wasted: when occupied with some familiar and semi-automatic task, such as dressing, washing up, mending socks, or digging in the garden; when walking or driving, when waiting in a bus queue or a traffic jam; in a moment of quiet before some especially painful or difficult interview; when unable to sleep, or before we have gained full consciousness on waking. Part of the distinctive value of the Jesus Prayer lies precisely in the fact that, because of its radical simplicity, it can be prayed in conditions of distraction when more complex forms of prayer are impossible. It is especially helpful in moments of tension and grave anxiety.

This 'free' use of the Jesus Prayer enables us to bridge the gap between our explicit 'times of prayer'—whether at church services or alone in our own room—and the normal activities of daily life. 'Pray without ceasing', St. Paul insists (1 Thess. 5:17): but how is this possible, since we have many other things to do as well? Bishop Theophan indicates the true method in his maxim, 'The hands at work, the mind and heart with God'.[1] The Jesus Prayer, becoming by frequent repetition almost habitual and unconscious, helps us to stand in the presence of God wherever we are—not only in the sanctuary or in solitude, but in the kitchen, on the factory floor, in the office. So we become like Brother Lawrence, who 'was more united with God during his ordinary activities than in religious exercises'. 'It is a great delusion', he remarked, 'to imagine that prayer-time should be different from any other, for we are equally bound to be united to God by work at work-time as by prayer at prayer-time.'[2]

This 'free' recitation of the Jesus Prayer is complemented and strengthened by the 'formal' use, when we concentrate our whole attention on the saying of the Prayer, to the exclusion of all external activity. Here, again, there are no rigid rules, but variety and flexibility. No

---

1 *The Art of Prayer*, p. 92.
2 Brother Lawrence of the Resurrection (1611-91), Barefooted Carmelite, *The Practice of the Presence of God*, ed. D. Attwater (Paraclete Books, London 1962), pp. 13, 16.

particular posture is essential. In Orthodox practice the Prayer is most usually recited when seated, but it may also be said standing or kneeling—and even, in cases of bodily weakness and physical exhaustion, when lying down. It is normally recited in complete darkness or with the eyes closed, not with open eyes before an icon illuminated by candles or a votive lamp. *Starets* Silouan of Mount Athos (1866-1938), when saying the Prayer, used to stow his clock away in a cupboard so as not to hear it ticking, and then pull his thick woollen monastic cap over his eyes and ears.[1]

Darkness, however, can have a soporific effect! If we become drowsy as we sit or kneel reciting the Prayer, then we should stand up for a time, make the Sign of the Cross at the end of each Prayer, and then bend from the waist in a deep bow, touching the ground with the fingers of the right hand. We may even make a prostration each time, touching the ground with our forehead. When reciting the Prayer seated, we should ensure that the chair is not too comfortable; preferably it should have no arms or back. The Prayer may also be recited standing with arms outstretched in the form of a cross.

A prayer-rope or rosary (*komvoschoinion, tchotki*), normally with a hundred knots, is often employed in conjunction with the Prayer, not primarily in order to count the number of times it is repeated, but rather as an aid to concentration and the establishment of a regular rhythm. Quantitative measurement, whether with a prayer-rope or in other ways, is not encouraged. It is true that, in the early part of *The Way of a Pilgrim*, great emphasis is laid by the *starets* on the precise number of times that the Prayer is to be said daily: 3,000 times, increasing to 6,000, and then to 12,000. The Pilgrim is commanded to say an exact number, neither more nor less. Such an attention to quantity is altogether unusual. Possibly the point here is not the sheer quantity but the inward attitude of the Pilgrim: the *starets* wishes to test his obedience and readiness to fulfil an appointed rule without deviation. More typical is the advice of Bishop Theophan: 'Do not trouble about the number of times you say the Prayer. Let this be your sole concern, that it should spring up in your heart with quickening power like a fountain of living water. Expel entirely from your mind all thoughts of quantity.'[2]

1 Archimandrite Sofrony, *The Undistorted Image: Staretz Silouan* (London 1958), pp. 40-41.
2 Quoted in E. Behr-Sigel, 'La Prière à Jésus ou le mystère de la spiritualité monastique orthodoxe', *Dieu Vivant* 8 (1947), p. 81.

The Prayer is sometimes recited in groups, but more commonly alone; the words may be said aloud or silently. In Orthodox usage, when recited aloud it is spoken rather than chanted. There should be nothing forced or laboured in the recitation. The words should not be formed with excessive emphasis or inward violence, but the Prayer should be allowed to establish its own rhythm and accentuation, so that in time it comes to 'sing' within us by virtue of its own intrinsic melody. *Starets* Parfenii of Kiev likened the flowing movement of the Prayer to a gently murmuring stream.[1]

From all this it can be seen that the Invocation of the Name is a prayer for all seasons. It can be used by everyone, in every place and at every time. It is suitable for the 'beginner' as well as the more experienced; it can be offered in company with others or alone; it is equally appropriate in the desert or the city, in surroundings of recollected tranquillity or in the midst of the utmost noise and agitation. It is never out of place.

Completeness

Theologically, as the Russian Pilgrim rightly claims, the Jesus Prayer 'holds in itself the whole gospel truth'; it is 'a summary of the Gospels'.[2] In one brief sentence it embodies the two chief mysteries of the Christian faith, the Incarnation and the Trinity. It speaks, first, of the two natures of Christ the God-man (*Theanthropos*): of His humanity, for He is invoked by the human name, 'Jesus', which His Mother Mary gave to Him after His birth in Bethlehem; of His eternal Godhead, for He is also styled 'Lord' and 'Son of God'. In the second place, the Prayer speaks by implication, although not explicitly, of the three Persons of the Trinity. While addressed to the second Person, Jesus, it points also to the Father, for Jesus is called 'Son of God'; and the Holy Spirit is equally present in the Prayer, for 'no man cay say "Lord Jesus", except in the Holy Spirit' (1 Cor. 12:3). So the Jesus Prayer is both Christocentric and Trinitarian.

Devotionally, it is no less comprehensive. It embraces the two chief 'moments' of Christian devotion: the 'moment' of adoration, of looking up to God's glory and reaching out to Him in love; and the 'moment' of penitence, the sense of unworthiness and sin. There is a circular movement within the Prayer, a sequence of ascent and return. In the first half of the Prayer we rise up to God: 'Lord Jesus Christ, Son of God . . .'; and then

1 *The Art of Prayer*, p. 110.
2 *The Way of a Pilgrim*, tr. R.M. French (London 1954), p. 29.

in the second half we return to ourselves in compunction: '. . . have mercy on me a sinner'. 'Those who have tasted the gift of the Spirit', it is stated in the Macarian Homilies, 'are conscious of two things at the same time: on the one hand, of joy and consolation; on the other, of trembling and fear and mourning.'[1] Such is the inward dialectic of the Jesus Prayer.

These two 'moments'—the vision of divine glory and the consciousness of human sin—are united and reconciled in a third 'moment' as we pronounce the word 'mercy'. 'Mercy' denotes the bridging of the gulf between the righteousness of God and the fallen creation. He who says to God, 'Have mercy', laments his own helplessness, but voices at the same time a cry of hope. He speaks not only of sin but of its overcoming. He affirms that God in His glory accepts us though we are sinners, asking from us in return to accept the fact that we are accepted. So the Jesus Prayer contains not only a call to repentance but an assurance of forgiveness and salvation. The heart of the Prayer—the actual name 'Jesus'—bears precisely the sense of salvation: 'Thou shalt call His name Jesus, for He shall save His people from their sins' (Matt. 1:21). While there is sorrow for sin in the Jesus Prayer, it is not a hopeless but a 'joy-creating sorrow', in the phrase of St. John Climacus († c. 649).

Such are among the riches, both theological and devotional, present in the Jesus Prayer; present, moreover, not merely in the abstract but in a vivifying and dynamic form. The special value of the Jesus Prayer lies in the fact that it makes these truths come alive, so that they are apprehended not just externally and theoretically but with all the fullness of our being. To understand why the Jesus Prayer possesses such efficacy, we must turn to two further aspects: the power of the Name and the discipline of repetition.

The power of the Name

'The Name of the Son of God is great and boundless, and upholds the entire universe.' So it is affirmed in The Shepherd of Hermas,[2] nor shall we appreciate the role of the Jesus Prayer in Orthodox spirituality unless we feel some sense of the intrinsic power and virtue of the divine Name. If the Jesus Prayer is more effective than other invocations, this is because it contains the Name of God.

1 Macarius/Symeon, Homily B25 (Dörries): in MS. Vatic. gr. 694, f. 149r.
2 Similitudes, ix, 14.

In the Old Testament,[1] as in other ancient cultures, there is a virtual identity between a man's soul and his name. His whole personality, with all its peculiarities and all its energy, is present in his name. To know a person's name is to gain a definite insight into his nature, and thereby to acquire an established relationship with him—even, perhaps, a certain control over him. That is why the mysterious messenger who wrestles with Jacob at the ford Jabbok refuses to disclose his name (Gen. 32:29). The same attitude is reflected in the reply of the angel to Manoah, 'Why askest thou thus after my name, seeing it is secret?' (Judg. 13:18). A change of name indicates a decisive change in a man's life, as when Abram becomes Abraham (Gen. 17:5), or Jacob becomes Israel (Gen. 32:28). In the same way, Saul after his conversion becomes Paul (Acts 13:9); and a monk at his profession is given a new name, usually not of his own choosing, to indicate the radical renewal which he undergoes.

In the Hebrew tradition, to do a thing *in the name* of another, or to *invoke* and *call upon his name*, are acts of the utmost weight and potency. To invoke a person's name is to make that person effectively present. 'One makes a name alive by mentioning it. The name immediately calls forth the soul it designates; therefore there is such deep significance in the very mention of a name.'[2]

Everything that is true of human names is true to an incomparably higher degree of the divine Name. The power and glory of God are present and active in His Name. The Name of God is *numen praesens*, God with us, *Emmanuel*. Attentively and deliberately to invoke God's Name is to place oneself in His presence, to open oneself to His energy, to offer oneself as an instrument and a living sacrifice in His hands. So keen was the sense of the majesty of the divine Name in later Judaism that the *tetragrammaton* was not pronounced aloud in the worship of the synagogue: the Name of the Most High was considered too devastating to be spoken.[3]

This Hebraic understanding of the Name passes from the Old Testament into the New. Devils are cast out and men are healed through the Name of

---

1 See J. Pederson, *Israel*, vol. i (London/Copenhagen 1926), pp. 245—59.

2 *Ibid.*, p. 256.

3 For the veneration of the Name among medieval Jewish Kabbalists, see Gershom G. Scholem, *Major Trends in Jewish Mysticism* (3rd ed., London 1955), pp. 132-3; and compare the treatment of this theme in the remarkable novel of Charles Williams, *All Hallows' Eve* (London 1945).

Jesus, for the Name is power. Once this potency of the Name is properly appreciated, many familiar passages acquire a fuller meaning and force: the clause in the Lord's Prayer, 'Hallowed be Thy Name'; Christ's promise at the Last Supper, 'Whatever you shall ask the Father in My Name, He will give it you' (John 16:23); His final command to the Apostles, 'Go therefore, and teach all nations, baptizing them in the Name of the Father, and of the Son, and of the Holy Spirit' (Matt. 28:19); St. Peter's proclamation that there is salvation only in 'the Name of Jesus Christ of Nazareth' (Acts 4:10-12); the words of St. Paul, 'At the Name of Jesus every knee should bow' (Phil. 2:10); the new and secret name written on the white stone which is given to us in the Age to Come (Rev. 2:17).

It is this biblical reverence for the Name that forms the basis and foundation of the Jesus Prayer. God's Name is essentially linked with His Person, and so the Invocation of the divine Name possesses a genuinely sacramental character, serving as an effective sign of His invisible presence and action. For the believing Christian today, as in apostolic times, the Name of Jesus is power. In the words of the two Elders of Gaza, St. Barsanuphius and St. John (sixth century), 'The remembrance of the Name of God utterly destroys all that is evil.'[1] 'Flog your enemies with the Name of Jesus', urges St. John Climacus, 'for there is no weapon more powerful in heaven or on earth. . . . Let the remembrance of Jesus be united to your every breath, and then you will know the value of stillness.'[2]

The Name is power, but a purely mechanical repetition will by itself achieve nothing. The Jesus Prayer is not a magic talisman. As in all sacramental operations, man is required to co-operate with God through his active faith and ascetic effort. We are called to invoke the Name with recollection and inward vigilance, confining our minds within the words of the Prayer, conscious who it is that we are addressing and that responds to us in our heart. Such strenuous prayer is never easy in the initial stages, and is rightly described by the Fathers as a hidden martyrdom. St. Gregory of Sinai speaks repeatedly of the 'constraint and labour' undergone by those who follow the Way of the Name; a 'continual effort' is needed; they will be tempted to give up 'because of the insistent pain that comes

---

1 *Questions and Answers*, ed. Sotirios Schoinas (Volos 1960), 693; tr. L. Regnault and P. Lemaire (Solesmes 1972), 692.
2 *Ladder*, 21 and 27 (PG 88, 945C and 1112C).

from the inward invocation of the mind'. 'Your shoulders will ache and you will often feel pain in your head,' he warns, 'but persevere persistently and with ardent longing, seeking the Lord in your heart.'[1] Only through such patient faithfulness shall we discover the true power of the Name.

This faithful perseverance takes the form, above all, of attentive and frequent repetition. Christ told His disciples not to use 'vain repetitions' (Matt. 6:7); but the repetition of the Jesus Prayer, when performed with inward sincerity and concentration, is most emphatically not 'vain'. The act of repeatedly invoking the Name has a double effect: it makes our prayer more unified and at the same time more inward.

Unification

As soon as we make a serious attempt to pray in spirit and in truth, at once we become acutely conscious of our inward disintegration, of our lack of unity and wholeness. In spite of all our efforts to stand before God, thoughts continue to move restlessly and aimlessly through our head, like the buzzing of flies (Bishop Theophan) or the capricious leaping of monkeys from branch to branch (Ramakrishna). To contemplate means, first of all, to be present where one is—to be *here* and *now*. But usually we find ourselves unable to restrain our mind from wandering at random over time and space. We recall the past, we anticipate the future, we plan what to do next; people and places come before us in unending succession. We lack the power to gather ourselves into the one place where we should be— *here*, in the presence of God; we are unable to live fully in the only moment of time that truly exists—*now*, the immediate present. This interior disintegration is one of the most tragic consequences of the Fall. The people who get things done, it has been justly observed, are the people who do one thing at a time. But to do one thing at a time is no mean achievement. While difficult enough in external work, it is harder still in the work of inward prayer.

What is to be done? How shall we learn to live in the present, in the eternal Now? How can we seize the *kairos*, the decisive moment, the moment of opportunity? It is precisely over this that the Jesus Prayer can help. The repeated Invocation of the Name can bring us, by God's grace, from dividedness to unity, from dispersion and multiplicity to singleness. 'To stop the continual jostling of your thoughts,' says Bishop Theophan,

---

1   See Kallistos Ware, 'The Jesus Prayer in St. Gregory of Sinai', *art. cit.*, pp. 14-15.

'you must bind the mind with one thought, or the thought of One only.'[1]

The ascetic Fathers, in particular Barsanuphius and John, distinguish two ways of combatting thoughts. The first method is for the 'strong' or the 'perfect'. These can 'contradict' their thoughts, that is, confront them face to face and repel them in direct battle. But for most of us such a method is too difficult and may, indeed, lead to actual harm. Direct confrontation, the attempt to uproot and expel thoughts by an effort of will, often serves merely to give greater strength to our imagination. Violently suppressed, our fantasies tend to return with increased force. Instead of fighting our thoughts directly and trying to eliminate them by an effort of will, it is wiser to turn aside and fix our attention elsewhere. Rather than gazing downwards into our turbulent imagination and concentrating on opposing our thoughts, we should look upwards to the Lord Jesus and entrust ourselves into His hands by invoking His Name; and the grace that acts through His Name will overcome the thoughts which we cannot obliterate by our own strength. Our spiritual strategy should be positive and not negative : instead of trying to empty our mind of what is evil, we should fill it with the thought of what is good. 'Do not contradict the thoughts suggested by your enemies,' advise Barsanuphius and John, 'for that is exactly what they want and they will not cease from troubling you. But turn to the Lord for help against them, laying before Him your own powerlessness; for He is able to expel them and to reduce them to nothing.'[2]

The Jesus Prayer, then, is a way of turning aside and looking elsewhere. Thoughts and images inevitably occur to us during prayer. We cannot stop their flow by a simple exertion of our will. It is of little or no value to say to ourselves, 'Stop thinking'; we might as well say, 'Stop breathing'. 'The rational mind cannot rest idle', says St. Mark the Monk;[3] thoughts keep filling it with ceaseless chatter, as in the dawn chorus of birds. But while we cannot make this chatter suddenly disappear, what we can do is to detach ourselves from it by 'binding' our ever-active mind 'with one thought, or the thought of One only'—the Name of Jesus. In the words of St. Diadochus (fifth century), 'When we have blocked all the outlets of the

---

1 *The Art of Prayer*, p. 97.

2 *Questions and Answers*, ed. Schoinas, 91; tr. Regnault and Lemaire, 166.

3 *On Penitence*, 11 (PG 65, 981B). The Greek text in Migne requires emendation here.

mind by means of the remembrance of God, then it requires of us at all costs some task which will satisfy its need of activity. Let us give it, then, as its sole activity the invocation *Lord Jesus* . . .'[1] 'Through the remembrance of Jesus Christ', states Philotheos of Sinai (?ninth-tenth century), 'gather together your disintegrated mind that is scattered abroad.'[2] Instead, then, of trying to halt the sequence of thoughts through our own power, we rely on the power that acts through the Name.

According to Evagrius of Pontus (†399), 'Prayer is a laying aside of thoughts.'[3] *A laying aside*: not a savage conflict, not a furious repression, but a gentle yet persistent act of detachment. Through the repetition of the Name, we are helped to 'lay aside', to 'let go', our trivial or pernicious imaginings, and to replace them with the thought of Jesus. But, although the imagination and the discursive reasoning are not to be violently suppressed when saying the Jesus Prayer, they are certainly not to be actively encouraged. The Jesus Prayer is not a form of meditation upon specific incidents in the life of Christ, or upon some saying or parable in the Gospels; still less is it a way of reasoning and inwardly debating about some theological truth such as the meaning of *homoousios* or the Chalcedonian Definition. In this regard, the Jesus Prayer is to be sharply distinguished from the methods of discursive meditation popular in the West since the Counter-Reformation (Ignatius Loyola, François de Sales, Alphonsus Liguori, etc.).

As we invoke the Name, we should not deliberately shape in our minds any visual image of the Saviour. This is one of the reasons why we say the Prayer in darkness, rather than with our eyes open in front of an icon. 'Keep your mind free from colours, images and forms', urges St. Gregory of Sinai; beware of the imagination (*phantasia*) in prayer—otherwise you may find that you have become a *phantastes* instead of a *hesychastes*![4] 'So as not to fall into illusion (*prelest*) while practising inner prayer,' states St. Nil Sorskii (†1508), 'do not permit yourself any concepts, images or visions.'[5] 'Hold no intermediate image between the mind and the Lord when practising the Jesus Prayer', Bishop Theophan writes. '. . . The

1 *A Hundred Texts on Knowledge and Discernment,* 59 (ed. E. des Places, *Sources chrétiennes,* 5bis [Paris 1955], p.119).
2 *Chapters,* 27 (*Philokalia,* vol. ii [Athens 1958], p. 283).
3 *On Prayer,* 70 (PG 79, 1181C).
4 *How the hesychast should persevere in prayer,* 7 (PG 150, 1340D).
5 *The Art of Prayer,* p. 101.

essential part is to dwell in God, and this walking before God means that you live with the conviction ever before your consciousness that God is in you, as He is in everything: you live in the firm assurance that He sees all that is within you, knowing you better than you know yourself. This awareness of the eye of God looking at your inner being *must not be accompanied by any visual concept, but must be confined to a simple conviction or feeling.*[1] Only when we invoke the Name in this way—not forming pictures of the Saviour but simply *feeling* His presence—shall we experience the full power of the Jesus Prayer to integrate and unify.

Inwardness

The repeated Invocation of the Name, by making our prayer more unified, makes it at the same time more inward, more a part of ourselves—not something that we *do* at particular moments, but something that we *are* all the time; not an occasional act but a continuing state. Such praying becomes truly prayer of the *whole man*, in which the words and meaning of the prayer are fully identified with the one who prays. All this is well expressed by the late Paul Evdokimov (1901-70): 'In the catacombs the image that recurs most frequently is the figure of a woman in prayer, the *Orans*. It represents the only true attitude of the human soul. It is not enough to *possess* prayer: we must *become* prayer—prayer incarnate. It is not enough to have moments of praise; our whole life, every act and every gesture, even a smile, must become a hymn of adoration, an offering, a prayer. We must offer not what we *have* but what we *are*.'[2] That is what the world needs above all else: not people who *say* prayers with greater or less regularity, but people who *are* prayers.

The kind of prayer that Evdokimov is here describing may be defined more exactly as 'prayer of the heart'. In Orthodoxy, as in many other traditions, prayer is commonly distinguished into three categories, which are to be regarded as interpenetrating levels rather than successive stages: prayer of the lips (oral prayer); prayer of the mind (mental prayer); prayer of the heart (or of the mind in the heart). The Invocation of the Name begins, like any other prayer, as an oral prayer, in which words are spoken by the tongue through a deliberate effort of will. At the same time, once more by a deliberate effort, we concentrate our mind upon the meaning of

1 *The Art of Prayer*, p. 100.

2 *Sacrement de l'amour. Le mystère conjugal à la lumière de la tradition orthodoxe* (Paris 1962), p. 83.

what the tongue says. In course of time and with the help of God our prayer grows more inward. The participation of the mind becomes more intense and spontaneous, while the sounds uttered by the tongue become less important; perhaps for a time they cease altogether and the Name is invoked silently, without any movement of the lips, by the mind alone. When this occurs, we have passed by God's grace from the first level to the second. Not that vocal invocation ceases altogether, for there will be times when even the most 'advanced' in inward prayer will wish to call upon the Lord Jesus aloud. (And who, indeed, can claim to be 'advanced'? We are all of us 'beginners' in the things of the Spirit.)

But the journey inwards is not yet complete. A man is far more than his conscious mind; besides his brain and reasoning faculties there are his emotions and affections, his aesthetic sensitivity, together with the deep instinctive layers of his personality. All these have a function to perform in prayer, for the whole man is called to share in the total act of worship. Like a drop of ink that falls on blotting paper, the act of prayer should spread steadily outwards from the conscious and reasoning centre of the brain, until it embraces every part of ourselves.

In more technical terms, this means that we are called to advance from the second level to the third: from 'prayer of the mind' to 'prayer of the mind in the heart'. 'Heart' in this context is to be understood in the Semitic and biblical rather than the modern sense, as signifying not just the emotions and affections but the totality of the human person. The heart is the primary organ of man's being, the innermost man, 'the very deepest and truest self, not attained except through sacrifice, through death'.[1] According to B. Vysheslavtsev, it is 'the centre not only of consciousness but of the unconscious, not only of the soul but of the spirit, not only of the spirit but of the body, not only of the comprehensible but of the incomprehensible; in one word, it is the absolute centre'.[2] Interpreted in this way, the heart is far more than a material organ in the body; the physical heart is an outward symbol of the boundless spiritual potentialities of the human creature, made in the image and likeness of God.

1 Richard Kehoe, OP, 'The Scriptures as Word of God', *The Eastern Churches Quarterly* viii (1947), supplementary issue on 'Tradition and Scripture', p. 78.

2 Quoted in John B. Dunlop, *Staretz Amvrosy: Model for Dostoevsky's Staretz Zossima* (Belmont, Mass., 1972), p. 22.

To accomplish the journey inwards and to attain true prayer, it is necessary to enter into this 'absolute centre', that is, to descend from the mind into the heart. More exactly, we are called to descend not from but *with* the mind. The aim is not just 'prayer of the heart' but 'prayer of the mind in the heart', for our conscious forms of understanding, including our reason, are a gift from God and are to be used in His service, not rejected. This 'union of the mind with the heart' signifies the reintegration of man's fallen and fragmented nature, his restoration to original wholeness. Prayer of the heart is a return to Paradise, a reversal of the Fall, a recovery of the *status ante peccatum*. This means that it is an eschatological reality, a pledge and anticipation of the Age to Come—something which, in this present age, is never fully and entirely realized.

Those who, however imperfectly, have achieved some measure of 'prayer of the heart', have begun to make the transition about which we spoke earlier—the transition from 'strenuous' to 'self-acting' prayer, from the prayer which I say to the prayer which 'says itself' or, rather, which Christ says in me. For the heart has a double significance in the spiritual life: it is both the centre of man's being and the point of meeting between man and God. It is both the place of self-knowledge, where man sees himself as he truly is, and the place of self-transcendence, where man understands his nature as a temple of the Holy Trinity, where the image comes face to face with the Archetype. In the 'inner chamber' of his own heart he finds the ground of his being and so crosses the mysterious frontier between the created and the Uncreated. 'There are unfathomable depths within the heart', state the Macarian Homilies. '. . . God is there with the angels, light and life are there, the kingdom and the apostles, the heavenly cities and the treasures of grace : all things are there.'[1]

Prayer of the heart, then, designates the point where 'my' action, 'my' prayer, becomes explicitly identified with the continuous action of Another in me. It is no longer prayer *to* Jesus but the prayer *of* Jesus Himself. This transition from 'strenuous' to 'self-acting' prayer is strikingly indicated in *The Way of a Pilgrim* : 'Early one morning the Prayer woke me up as it were.'[2] Hitherto the Pilgrim has been 'saying the Prayer'; now he finds that the Prayer 'says itself', even when he is asleep, for it has become united to the prayer of God within him.

1 *Hom.* xv, 32 and xliii, 7 (ed. Dörries/Klostermann/Kroeger [Berlin 1964], pp. 146, 289).

2 *The Way of a Pilgrim*, p. 14.

Readers of *The Way of a Pilgrim* may gain the impression that this passage from oral prayer to prayer of the heart is easily achieved, almost in a mechanical and automatic fashion. The Pilgrim, so it seems, attains self-acting prayer in a matter of a few weeks. It needs to be emphasized that his experience, while not unique,[1] is altogether exceptional. More usually prayer of the heart comes, if at all, only after a lifetime of ascetic striving. It is the free gift of God, bestowed as and when He will, and not the inevitable effect of some technique. St. Isaac the Syrian (seventh century) underlines the extreme rarity of the gift when he says that 'scarcely one in ten thousand' is counted worthy of the gift of pure prayer, and he adds: 'As for the mystery that lies beyond pure prayer, there is scarcely to be found a single man in each generation who has drawn near to this knowledge of God's grace.'[2]

One in ten thousand, one in a generation: while sobered by this warning, we should not be unduly discouraged. The path to the inner kingdom lies open before all, and all alike may travel some way along it. In the present age, few experience with any fullness the deeper mysteries of the heart, but very many receive in a more humble and intermittent way true glimpses of what is signified by spiritual prayer.

Breathing exercises

It is time to consider a controversial topic, where the teaching of the Byzantine Hesychasts is often misinterpreted—the role of the body in prayer.

The heart, it has been said, is the primary organ of man's being, the point of convergence between mind and matter, the centre alike of man's physical constitution and of his psychic and spiritual structure. Since the heart has this twofold aspect, at once visible and invisible, prayer of the heart is prayer of body as well as soul: only if it includes the body can it

---

1 *Starets* Silouan of Mount Athos (1866-1938) had only been practising the Jesus Prayer for three weeks before it descended into his heart and became unceasing. His biographer, Archimandrite Sofrony, rightly points out that this was a 'sublime and rare gift'; not until later did Father Silouan come to appreciate how unusual it was (*The Undistorted Image*, p. 24). For further discussion of this question, see Kallistos Ware, ' "Pray without Ceasing": The Ideal of Continual Prayer in Eastern Monasticism', *Eastern Churches Review* ii (1969), pp. 259-61.

2 *Mystic Treatises by Isaac of Nineveh*, translated by A.J. Wensinck (Amsterdam 1923), p. 113.

be truly prayer of the whole man. A human being, in the biblical view, is a psycho-somatic totality—not a soul imprisoned in a body and seeking to escape, but an integral unity of the two. The body is not just an obstacle to be overcome, a lump of matter to be ignored, but it has a positive part to play in the spiritual life and it is endowed with energies that can be harnessed for the work of prayer.

If this is true of prayer in general, it is true in a more specific way of the Jesus Prayer, since this is an invocation addressed precisely to God Incarnate, to the Word made flesh. Christ at His Incarnation took not only a human mind and will but a human body, and so He has made the *flesh* into an inexhaustible source of sanctification. How can this flesh, which the God-man has made Spirit-bearing, participate in the Invocation of the Name and in prayer of the mind in the heart?

To assist such participation, and as an aid to concentration, the Hesychasts evolved a 'physical technique'. Every psychic activity, they realized, has repercussions on the physical and bodily level; depending on our inward state we grow hot or cold, we breath faster or more slowly, the rhythm of our heart-beats quickens or decelerates, and so on. Conversely, each alteration in our physical condition reacts adversely or positively on our psychic activity. If, then, we can learn to control and regulate certain of our physical processes, this can be used to strengthen our inward concentration in prayer. Such is the basic principle of the Hesychast 'method'. In detail, their physical technique has three main aspects:

(i) *External posture*. St. Gregory of Sinai advises sitting on a low stool, about eight inches high; the head and shoulders should be bowed, and the eyes fixed on the place of the heart. He recognizes that this will prove exceedingly uncomfortable after a time. Some writers recommend a yet more exacting posture, with the head held between the knees, following the example of Elijah on Mount Carmel.[1]

(ii) *Control of the breathing*. The breathing is to be made slower and at the same time co-ordinated with the rhythm of the Prayer. Often the first part, 'Lord Jesus Christ, Son of God', is said while drawing in the breath, and the second part, 'have mercy on me, a sinner', while breathing out.

---

1 'Elijah climbed to the crest of Carmel. There he crouched to the ground with his face between his knees' (1 Kings 18:42). For an illustration of a monk praying in this position, taken from a Greek manuscript of the eleventh century, see J. Meyendorff, *St. Grégoire Palamas et la mystique orthodoxe* (Paris 1959), p. 92.

Other methods are possible. The recitation of the Prayer may also be synchronized with the beating of the heart.

(iii) *Inward Exploration.* Just as the aspirant in Yoga is taught to concentrate his thought in specific parts of his body, so the Hesychast concentrates his thought in the cardiac centre. While inhaling through his nose and propelling his breath down into his lungs, he makes his mind 'descend' with the breath and he 'searches' inwardly for the place of the heart. Exact instructions concerning this exercise are not committed to writing for fear they should be misunderstood; the details of the process are so delicate that the personal guidance of an experienced master is *indispensable.* The beginner who, in the absence of such guidance, attempts to search for the cardiac centre, is in danger of directing his thought unawares into the area which lies immediately below the heart— into the abdomen, that is, and the entrails. The effect on his prayer is disastrous, for this lower region is the source of the carnal thoughts and sensations which pollute the mind and the heart.[1]

For obvious reasons the utmost discretion is necessary when interfering with instinctive bodily activities such as the drawing of breath or the beating of the heart. Misuse of the physical technique can damage a man's health and disturb his mental equilibrium; hence the importance of a reliable master. If no such *starets* is available, it is best for the beginner to restrict himself simply to the actual recitation of the Jesus Prayer, without troubling at all about the rhythm of his breath or his heart-beats. More often than not he will find that, without any conscious effort on his part, the words of the Invocation adapt themselves spontaneously to the movement of his breathing and his heart. If this does not in fact happen, there is no cause for alarm; let him continue quietly with the work of mental invocation.

The physical techniques are in any case no more than an accessory, an aid which has proved helpful to some but which is in no sense obligatory upon all. The Jesus Prayer can be practised in its fullness without any physical methods at all. St. Gregory Palamas (1296-1359), while regarding the use of physical techniques as theologically defensible, treated such

---

1 For further bibliography on the control of the breathing, see Kallistos Ware, 'The Jesus Prayer in St. Gregory of Sinai', *art. cit.,* p. 14, note 55. On the various physical centres in man, and their spiritual implications, see Dr. André Bloom (now Metropolitan Anthony of Surozh), 'Contemplation et ascèse: contribution orthodoxe', in *Technique et contemplation (Etudes Carmélitaines,* no. 28: Bruges 1949), pp. 49-67.

methods as something secondary and suited mainly for beginners.[1] For him, as for all the Hesychast masters, the essential thing is not the external control of the breathing but the inward and secret Invocation of the Lord Jesus.

Orthodox writers in the last 150 years have in general laid little emphasis upon the physical techniques. The counsel given by Bishop Ignatii Brianchaninov (1807-67) is typical:

> We advise our beloved brethren not to try to establish this technique within them, if it does not reveal itself of its own accord. Many, wishing to learn it by experience, have damaged their lungs and gained nothing. The essence of the matter consists in the union of the mind with the heart during prayer, and this is achieved by the grace of God in its own time, determined by God. The breathing technique is fully replaced by the unhurried enunciation of the Prayer, by a short rest or pause at the end, each time it is said, by gentle and unhurried breathing, and by the enclosure of the mind in the words of the Prayer. By means of these aids we can easily attain to a certain degree of attention.[2]

As regards the speed of recitation, Bishop Ignatii suggests:

> To say the Jesus Prayer a hundred times attentively and without haste, about half an hour is needed; but some ascetics require even longer. Do not say the prayers hurriedly, one immediately after another. Make a short pause after each prayer, and so help the mind to concentrate. Saying the Prayer without pauses distracts the mind. Breathe with care, gently and slowly.[3]

Beginners in the use of the Prayer will probably prefer a somewhat faster pace than is here proposed—perhaps twenty minutes for a hundred Prayers.

Striking parallels exist between the physical techniques recommended by the Byzantine Hesychasts and those employed in Hindu Yoga and in

1 *Triads in defence of the Holy Hesychasts*, I, ii, 7 (ed. J. Meyendorff [Louvain 1959], vol. i, p.97).

2 *The Arena: An Offering to Contemporary Monasticism*, translated by Archimandrite Lazarus (Madras 1970), p. 84 (translation slightly altered).

3 *Op. cit.*, p. 81.

Sūfism.[1] How far are the similarities the result of mere coincidence, of an independent though analogous development in two separate traditions? If there is a direct relation between Hesychasm and Sūfism—and some of the parallels are so close that mere coincidence seems excluded—which side has been borrowing from the other? Here is a fascinating field for research, although the evidence is perhaps too fragmentary to permit any definite conclusion. One point, however, should not be forgotten. Besides similarities, there are also differences. All pictures have frames, and all picture-frames have certain features in common; yet the pictures within the frames may be utterly different. What matters is the picture, not the frame. In the case of the Jesus Prayer, the physical techniques are as it were the frame, while the mental invocation of Christ is the picture within the frame. The 'frame' of the Jesus Prayer certainly resembles various non-Christian 'frames', but this should not make us insensitive to the uniqueness of the picture within, to the distinctively Christian content of the Prayer. The essential point in the Jesus Prayer is not the act of repetition in itself, not how we sit or breathe, but *to whom* we speak; and in this instance the words are addressed unambiguously to the Incarnate Saviour Jesus Christ, Son of God and Son of Mary.

The existence of a physical technique in connection with the Jesus Prayer should not blind us as to the Prayer's true character. The Jesus Prayer is not just a device to help us concentrate or relax. It is not simply a piece of 'Christian Yoga', a type of 'Transcendental Meditation', or a 'Christian mantra', even though some have tried to interpret it in this way. It is, on the contrary, an invocation specifically *addressed to another person*—to God made man, Jesus Christ, our personal Saviour and Redeemer. The Jesus Prayer, therefore, is far more than an isolated method or technique. It exists within a certain context, and if divorced from that context it loses its proper meaning.

The context of the Jesus Prayer is first of all one of *faith*. The Invocation of the Name presupposes that the one who says the Prayer believes in Jesus Christ as Son of God and Saviour. Behind the repetition of a form of words there must exist a living faith in the Lord Jesus—in who He is and in what He has done for me personally. Perhaps the faith in many of us is

---

1 See L. Gardet, 'Un problème de mystique comparée: la mention du nom divin (*dhikr*) dans la mystique musulmane', *Revue Thomiste*, lii (1952), pp. 642-79; liii (1953), pp. 197-216.

very uncertain and faltering; perhaps it coexists with doubt; perhaps we often find ourselves compelled to cry out in company with the father of the lunatic child, 'Lord, I believe: help my unbelief.' (Mark 9:24.) But at least there should be some *desire* to believe; at least there should be, amidst all the uncertainty, a spark of love for the Jesus whom as yet we know so imperfectly.

Secondly, the context of the Jesus Prayer is one of *community*. We do not invoke the Name as separate individuals, relying solely upon our own inward resources, but as members of the community of the Church. Writers such as St. Barsanuphius, St. Gregory of Sinai or Bishop Theophan took it for granted that those to whom they commended the Jesus Prayer were baptized members of the Church, regularly participating in the Church's sacramental life through Confession and Holy Communion. Not for one moment did they envisage the Invocation of the Name as a substitute for the sacraments, but they assumed that anyone using it would be a practising and communicant member of the Church.

Yet today, in this present time of restless curiosity and ecclesiastical disintegration, there are in fact very many who use the Jesus Prayer without being practising members of any Church, possibly without having a clear faith either in the Lord Jesus or in anything else. Are we to condemn them? Are we to forbid them the use of the Prayer? Surely not, so long as they are sincerely searching for the Fountain of Life. Jesus condemned no one except hypocrites. But, in all humility and acutely aware of our own faithlessness, we are bound to regard the situation of such people as anomalous, and to warn them of this fact.

The journey's end

The aim of the Jesus Prayer, as of all Christian prayer, is that our praying should become increasingly identified with the prayer offered by Jesus the High Priest within us, that our life should become one with His life, our breathing with the Divine Breath that sustains the universe. The final objective may aptly be described by the Patristic term *theosis*, 'deification' or 'divinization'. In the words of Archpriest Sergei Bulgakov, 'The Name of Jesus, present in the human heart, confers upon it the power of deification.'[1] 'The Logos became man,' says St. Athanasius, 'that we might become God.'[2] He who is God by nature took our humanity, that

---

1 *The Orthodox Church* (London 1935), p.170 (translation altered).
2 *On the Incarnation*, 54.

we men might share by grace in His divinity, becoming 'partakers of the divine nature.' (2 Peter 1:4.) The Jesus Prayer, addressed to the Logos Incarnate, is a means of realizing within ourselves this mystery of *theosis*, whereby man attains to the true likeness of God.

The Jesus Prayer, by uniting us to Christ, helps us to share in the mutual indwelling or *perichoresis* of the three Persons of the Holy Trinity. The more the Prayer becomes a part of ourselves, the more we enter into the movement of love which passes unceasingly between Father, Son, and Holy Spirit. Of this love St. Isaac the Syrian has written with great beauty:

> Love is the kingdom of which our Lord spoke symbolically when He promised his disciples that they would eat in His kingdom: 'You shall eat and drink at the table of My kingdom.' What should they eat, if not love? . . . When we have reached love, we have reached God and our way is ended: we have passed over to the island that lies beyond the world, where is the Father with the Son and the Holy Spirit: to whom be glory and dominion.[1]

In the Hesychast tradition, the mystery of *theosis* has most often taken the outward form of a vision of light. This light which the saints behold in prayer is neither a symbolical light of the intellect, nor yet a physical and created light of the senses. It is nothing less than the divine and uncreated Light of the Godhead, which shone from Christ at His Transfiguration on Mount Tabor and which will illuminate the whole world at His second coming on the Last Day. Here is a characteristic passage on the Divine Light taken from St. Gregory Palamas. He is describing the Apostle's vision when he was caught up into the third heaven (2 Cor. 12:2-4):

> Paul saw a light without limits below or above or to the sides; he saw no limit whatever to the light that appeared to him and shone around him, but it was like a sun infinitely brighter and vaster than the universe; and in the midst of this sun he himself stood, having become nothing but eye.[2]

Such is the vision of glory to which we may approach through the Invocation of the Name. The Jesus Prayer causes the brightness of the Transfiguration to penetrate into every corner of our life. Constant repetition has two effects upon the anonymous author of *The Way of a*

1 *Mystic Treatises*, tr. Wensinck, pp.211-12.
2 *Triads in defence of the Holy Hesychasts*, I, iii, 21 (ed. Meyendorff, vol. i, p.157).

Pilgrim. First, it transforms his relationship with the material creation around him, making all things transparent, changing them into a sacrament of God's presence. He writes:

> When I prayed with my heart, everything around me seemed delightful and marvellous. The trees, the grass, the birds, the earth, the air, the light seemed to be telling me that they existed for man's sake, that they witnessed to the love of God for man, that everything proved the love of God for man, that all things prayed to God and sang His praise. Thus it was that I came to understand what *The Philokalia* calls 'the knowledge of the speech of all creatures' . . . I felt a burning love for Jesus Christ and for all God's creatures.[1]

In the words of Father Bulgakov, 'Shining through the heart, the light of the Name of Jesus illuminates all the universe.'[2]

In the second place, the Prayer transfigured the Pilgrim's relation not only with the material creation but with other men.

> Again I started off on my wanderings. But now I did not walk along as before, filled with care. The Invocation of the Name of Jesus gladdened my way. Everybody was kind to me, it was as though everyone loved me. . . . If anyone harms me I have only to think, 'How sweet is the Prayer of Jesus!' and the injury and the anger alike pass away and I forget it all.[3]

'Inasmuch as you have done it unto one of the least of these My brethren, you have done it unto Me.' (Matt. 25:40.) The Jesus Prayer helps us to see Christ in all men, and all men in Christ.

The Jesus Prayer, therefore, is not escapist and world-denying but, on the contrary, intensely affirmative. It does not imply a rejection of God's creation, but the reassertion of the ultimate value of everything and everyone in God. As Dr. Nadejda Gorodetzky says:

> We can apply this Name to people, books, flowers, to all things we meet, see or think. The Name of Jesus may become a mystical key to the world, an instrument of the hidden offering of everything and everyone, setting the divine seal on the world. One might perhaps speak here of the priesthood of all believers. In union with our High Priest, we

1 *The Way of a Pilgrim*, pp. 31-2, 41.
2 *The Orthodox Church*, p. 171.
3 *The Way of a Pilgrim*, pp. 17-18.

97

implore the Spirit: Make my prayer into a sacrament.[1]

'Prayer is action; to pray is to be highly effective.'[2] Of no prayer is this more true than of the Jesus Prayer. While it is singled out for particular mention in the office of monastic profession as a prayer for monks and nuns,[3] it is equally a prayer for laymen, for married couples, for doctors and psychiatrists, for social workers and bus conductors. The Invocation of the Name, practised aright, involves each one more deeply in his or her appointed task, making each more efficient in his actions, not cutting him off from others but linking him to them, rendering him sensitive to their fears and anxieties in a way that he never was before. The Jesus Prayer makes each into a 'man for others', a living instrument of God's peace, a dynamic centre of reconciliation.

---

1 'The Prayer of Jesus', *Blackfriars* xxiii (1942), p. 76.

2 Tito Colliander, *The Way of the Ascetics*, p. 71.

3 At the clothing of a monk, in both the Greek and the Russian practice, it is the custom to give him a prayer-rope (*komvoschoinion*). In the Russian use the abbot says the following as it is handed over: 'Take, brother, the sword of the Spirit, which is the Word of God, for continual prayer to Jesus; for you must always have the Name of the Lord Jesus in mind, in heart, and on your lips, ever saying: Lord Jesus Christ, Son of God, have mercy on me a sinner.' See N.F. Robinson, SSJE, *Monasticism in the Orthodox Churches* (London/Milwaukee 1916), pp. 159-60. Note the usual distinction between the three levels of prayer: lips, mind, heart.

PRAYER:

ENCOUNTERING THE DEPTHS

by

Mother Mary Clare SLG

I

None of us would question that prayer is concerned with a relationship, the relationship which exists between God and man, and that through this relationship man can experience the deep and satisfying 'belonging-together' which prayer provides. This relationship allows God to be God and man to be man—for this is man's freedom. In this context alone are God and man bound together, and in it we discover how the process of mutual exploration which is prayer may develop.

Prayer is a way of encounter. This is the Christian way. By his nature man is so constituted that he can only become fully himself as a person through the successful adjustment of his relationship with those realities other than himself amongst whom or in which his life is lived. He must face them and relate himself freely to them, not omitting any part of what he is or of what he can become conscious. This facing and balancing of the individual life to the tensions set up by the relationship is *encounter*. The development of relationship, at its highest level, is the nature and purpose of the life of prayer.

This fact, which is natural to man, is fulfilled and made perfect in Christ, for in Christ man is made free and is restored to his dignity as the creature co-operating in love with his Creator, so working out in time and space the Divine will—which is man's history.

As we all know, we cannot separate our relationship with God from our relationship with our fellow men, that is, our 'in depth person to person mutuality', a desire to be recognised as a person, leading to a movement away from a formalistic prayer life to a deep I-Thou relationship where in silence and solitude we meet God and in him are conscious of our coinherence in man's needs and sufferings. Through the modern media of communication and travel there is an ever expanding identification, not merely physical but also psychic, with the needs of everyone throughout the world. This knowledge must be redirected into and held by the conscious prayer of those who are channels of God's redemptive love—which is the real essence of intercessory prayer.

Openness to the Spirit

The second movement which has emerged in the prayer life of many is the type of prayer which moves into the Spirit who alone produces love. As St. Paul says in Galatians 5:32: 'The fruit of the Spirit is love . . .' which is, of course, relationship, and so the fruit of the Spirit builds up not only communion with God but the knowledge and true fellowship of community. Hence we have a movement towards 'shared prayer'. I do not want to go into this aspect of prayer in detail except to make the point that this prayer in common should not be seen as in opposition to deeper solitary prayer but rather as complementary to it. It is important to realise that in the rhythm of our prayer, as in the natural rhythm of our physical life as we pass through adolescence to full maturity, we may find that at times our prayer life will require more silence and withdrawal rather than shared prayer, while at other times the reverse might be true.

In both solitary and common prayer there is the desire to move away from surface impressions to deeper personal experiences, to get away from a de-personalised type of prayer life, whether individual or communal, and to extend this personal contact with God outwards, and this is always the test of its validity. But let us get the rhythm of our encounter entirely God-centred. When one moves away from the de-personalised type of formal meditation it must be to encounter the Holy Trinity—wherein the Father brings forth the Son, and the Son loves the Father in that bond of love which is the Spirit—for only so shall we be able to enter into that God-directed relationship which is the true ground for a charismatic openness to the Spirit.

Whatever may be our way of life this openness to the Spirit in prayer is possible, but it needs practice and perseverance in new beginnings; the will to pray, and times of 'pure prayer' when we do nothing else. Basically this disposition for prayer depends on our real givenness, an openness to Christ in us, and for this it is not essential to have a chapel, or even a 'holy corner' and a lighted candle as a focal point, though all these may help towards what may be called 'relaxed attention'. If we are to live in prayer, and this is true for the elementary beginner as well as for those who have had experience of the heights of contemplation, we must first and foremost let Christ pray in us and give him pride of place. To be perpetually conscious of this mysterious reality would probably be too much for the weakness of our human capacity. We can rightly and perhaps more safely be *un*conscious of the disposition of being always open to him, which is his gift. Let him work in the depths of ourselves, then every happening, every experience, however commonplace, can be brought to his Light, every event can receive his blessing, and be assessed from his point of view.

This goes deeper than the attempt, which we have all struggled to make in the past, to realise that our fellow men are indeed 'temples of the Holy Spirit', on account of which we have tried to put up with their idiosyncrasies and to love them in Christ. But have we not sometimes comforted ourselves with that well-known distinction which while theoretically requiring us to love our neighbour seems to permit us in practice to draw the line at *liking* our neighbour? But now the relationship is more than an effort at tolerance. It is a genuine love and reverence towards others, a respect for the uniqueness of each as God has created and loved each individually. 'I have loved you . . . I have called you by name . . . you are mine.' (Isaiah 43.) Now we have faith that God is working as uniquely in others' lives as we have experienced him in our own, so that the whole question of growth in prayer can be recognised for all in terms of the abiding presence of God.

The nature of contemplation
What then is contemplation? It is basically a looking towards God. Each one of us must get below the normal false ego into the very ground of our being where, to quote Julian of Norwich, 'we stand before God consciously turning towards him as the Source and Origin of our real selves.' In this sense contemplation is something applicable to every human being. Let me repeat this: the looking towards God is the essential act of contemplation. It is not having nice or pretty thoughts; it is not having a sensible realisation of his presence. It is the return of the whole being back to God, more often than not in the darkness of faith and in increasing dependency on the Spirit of God in prayer. St. Augustine said: 'He is more intimate to me than I am to myself', but that knowledge no one can reach by his own natural powers alone, because only God can reveal to any of us that he is the Source of our being.

This quiet contemplative dimension of faith is not vocal dialogue with God but a deeper knowledge that prayer leads us into a state of 'being', a stage of prayer that has superseded the use of our mental activity in which it was we who were doing the praying. Our prayer life has now moved into that stage of greater communication where there is an experience of the presence of God acting not through any sense or consolation but with the totality of his being, which cannot be pinned down to any idea or concept except that in all things we are in Christ in his offering to the Father by the power of the Holy Spirit. Thomas Merton reminds us that: 'The object of all Christian prayer is union with the Father, through the Person of the Son, by the Holy Spirit'; and again: 'All Christian prayer develops and becomes perfect by penetrating deeply, in the Spirit, into the hidden Mystery of Christ.'

So we find ourselves prostrate before this great mystery and begin to understand more humbly that in contemplation God himself has provided the way to a life of union. It is no longer a question of search, a balancing of philosophies, discriminating between differing systems or deciding between claims of revelation; for God in flesh has said: 'The hour cometh, and now is, when the true worshippers shall worship the Father in spirit and in truth; for the Father seeketh such to worship him. God is a Spirit, and they that worship him must worship in spirit and in truth.' (John 4:23-24.) Here is the absolute claim of God, and one that has the greatest force in bringing about a deep and lasting *metanoia* in our lives. 'By their fruits you shall know them' is the only criterion of the reality of our prayer life.

I should like to relate what I have tried to express about prayer to the climate of the times in which we live, for we must be increasingly aware that many of the traditional forms of Christian prayer do not seem to be relevant to the rising generation. I have deliberately spoken, to use Teresian language, of the heights of Christian contemplation because the 'nomad' of today has not merely struck his material tents in order to move from the complexity of a broken-down and over-ripe civilisation into the deserts of a simple primitive life, but there is a nomad mentality which is seeking for a new statement of the purpose of man's very nature, a mentality for which all traditions are suspect and inadequate.

It is a period in which every part of human activity is in a phase of crisis—economic, political, philosophical and religious. The foundations of Christian thought and revelation are being laid bare and amid contradictory interpretations many are saying in despair, 'What is truth?' and are hesitating to commit themselves to traditional forms of religious observance.

Prayer as the search for personal union with God

More than ever, therefore, prayer must not be put forward as a technique to be mastered by the few, but rather as the heritage of all, the essential means of living the Christian life and coming to that personal union with God for which we were created. To quote Thomas Merton again: 'Whoever we are, whatever may be our state of life, we are called to the glory and freedom of the sons of God. Our vocation is union with Christ. We are co-heirs with him of his own divine glory. We share his divine Sonship . . . Therefore when you and I become what we are really meant to be, we will discover not only that we love one another perfectly but that we are both living in Christ and Christ in us, and we are all One Christ. We will see that it is he who loves in us.' [1]

It is a baffling fact that today we frequently find that the true God-seekers, with a hunger and thirst for guidance in silence and the reality of prayer, are to be found outside the orbit of institutional religion. All the more do we need to be very clear that in our own concepts of renewal we do not lose the spirit of silence and of God-awareness just because the old traditional forms of devotion seem to be outmoded. Many feel some inner urge or desire for knowledge of the spiritual and ask how, through ordered Christian practice and tradition, they can find that for which the heart of man is seeking. It is the old question: 'Art thou he that should come, or do we look for another?' (Matthew 11:13.)

Modern man is the descendant of the Renaissance in which man rediscovered himself, while the Pelagianism which lay dormant in the Middle Ages has again emerged and man thinks that he may find the solution of his ultimate purpose by studying man. The Christian can rightly be grateful both for the scepticism of the scientific temper and also for what the scientific and the psychological methods have discovered about the nature of human personality. The modern Christian should approach both his study of the relevance of religion and also his practice of prayer in the light of such criticism and information. At the same time—or rather, perhaps, following on by way of reaction to the scientific and psychological ethos of our era—there has emerged a widespread interest in eastern spirituality. But because we are learning to recognise the riches that the sages have acquired by the rivers of India, there is no need to ignore the revelation of God by the banks of the Jordan; and you will forgive me if I say it might be unwise to mix the waters indiscriminately, though each stream of spirituality can stimulate the other. Indeed, one interesting example of this stimulation of one stream by another can be seen in an experiment made by a Cistercian abbey in America—St. Joseph's Abbey, Mass.—when they invited a Zen master to conduct their retreat on Zen lines. The master had studied Christianity deeply and when the retreat began, to their surprise, he gave them koans (enigmatic sayings which trigger off meditation) drawn from the Christian Scriptures. The aim of the meditation on these koans is not so much to understand the answer as to experience it. When they came to interviews with him they found themselves sent back again and again to think more deeply, to go ever deeper into the truth. Fr. Basil Pennington, commenting on this, says: 'We might learn from our Zen master to take but one bit at a time, one Christian koan, and struggle with it until we have truly not only seen every facet of it, explained it in every direction, but have experienced its reality. This, and this alone, leads to true contemplation—not thought or thoughts, but wonder, questioning, searching, opening, until finally we experience reality—*the* Reality.' [2]

It is by all such means that we may gain a clear message of the Spirit to offer to those who come to us, for to accept the Christian fundamental 'Very God of very God' merely as a clause in a creed is not sufficient. Faith is not faith if it is only an intellectual belief that certain propositions are true, and that, in consequence, certain standards of conduct are desirable. Faith, as the Old Testament speaks of it, and as the saints inspired by the New have experienced it, is a total commitment of person to Person. It is more than reliance on mercy and forgiveness, or the most devoted admiration of the idealist. It must be a response to the Divine Personality so that there is a knitting together of persons—the Lover and the beloved. And because love is of the will it is, therefore, a work of the will, blossoming into the fullness of charity. The crisis of today is, more than anything else, a test of faith: 'See that ye refuse not him that speaketh . . . whose voice then shook the earth: but now he has promised saying, Yet once more I shake not the earth only, but also heaven. And this word, Yet once more, signifieth the removing of those things that are shaken . . . that those things that cannot be shaken may remain.' (Hebrews 12:25-27.)

Prayer as God's activity in us

This intimacy and firmness of faith in our Lord is brought about through the interchange and communication of prayer. It is in prayer that the will of God is made known. It is in prayer that the soul is enabled to make its mature response to his will. It is in prayer that the soul finds itself truly in God, with its latent possibilities sanctified in his life. In prayer there is indeed a variety of calling and experience, but there is a common obligation. To abandon prayer is equivalent to suicide in the physical life; to regard prayer as unchanging and without need of development is equivalent to being a fixed adolescent. As Thomas Merton says in *Contemplation in a World of Action:* 'What has to be rediscovered is the inner discipline of "the heart", that is to say, of the "whole man"—a discipline that reaches down into his inmost ground and opens out to the invisible, intangible, but nevertheless mysteriously sensible reality of God's presence, of his love, and of his activity in our hearts.'

We must therefore grow in the life of the Spirit, and we shall do that most effectively by total openness, like Mary the mother of God: 'Behold the handmaid of the Lord'—for this is contemplation. There we see in her not passivity in the negative sense but a passivity which is resisting her own activity and in which her whole being is actively receiving God's activity. In other words, we must be passive to the natural that it may be flooded with the spiritual, and active to the spiritual that it may descend into the natural. It is a terrific activity and a tremendous passivity in which the whole being is impenetrated by the life of the Spirit.

We have an increasing need not only in our prayer but also in our actions to become unified and simplified. This is the true redirection of the perceptions of memory and imagination which gathers our whole being to the one point where God is no longer an object exterior to ourselves but one who is intimately present within us. Through this new dimension a whole new world can and does open up to us, and faith becomes a living reality and many things, even in the natural world, which we did not observe before are seen to be expressions of God's activity, so that having passed through the darkness of faith we can enter into that richness of possessing all things in Christ as expressed in St. John of the Cross's affirmation:

'The heavens are mine, the earth is mine and the nations are mine; mine are the just, and the sinners are mine; mine are the angels, the Mother of God is mine, and all things are mine; God himself is mine and for me, because Christ is mine and all for me.' *(Maxims)*

Every prayer is for God's sake, for his glory; every prayer is obedience to God in Christ. We must let Christ pray in us that he may in us unceasingly make an offering of the world 'ever and ever new again'. (Orthodox Liturgy.) Such prayer is a giving of ourselves, for it is independent of us, of what we know or do not know, what we want or do not want; it is an offering, seeking nothing for self, and it is an act of self-consecration to God when we forego control and power of analysis. We come empty-handed, with no security, knowing neither success or failure—God is central and our attention is given to him. Prayer like this goes on in the depths—understanding, will, feeling, register nothing and control nothing.

When we know that we desire to live in prayer we realise that we are called to go a certain way. We have not yet reached the goal, and are, indeed, only at the beginning of something which will not be complete until Eternity. Prayer is for us always an adventure in which God is continually converting us to himself, and drawing us into his new creation, ourselves and the whole world, which we represent when we pray. This is our aim: to be open to respond to his action in us, to persevere in trying to do his will, and not to weary of praying for the gift of the Holy Spirit and of prayer so that we may truly let Christ pray in the depths of our being.

II

We have considered the depths of the mystery of God in relation to ourselves and our times. We have glimpsed the glorious potential that is ours through our union with God in Christ by the power of the Spirit. This 'mystery of the unsearchable riches of Christ' of which St. Paul speaks in the letter to the Ephesians (3:8) is made known to us and through us here and now and is also the measure of our prayer for one another, so that our relationships can be expressed in the words of St. Paul, 'that you being rooted and grounded in love, may have power to comprehend with all the saints what is the breadth and length and height and depth and to know the love of Christ which surpasses all knowledge, that you may be filled with all the fullness of God.' (Eph. 3:17-19.)

But to leave it there is not enough, even as it was not enough for St. Paul. At the end of the same letter to the Ephesians he changes the language of adoration for that of conflict: 'Finally, my brethren, be strong in the Lord, and in the power of his might. Put on the whole armour of God, that you may be able to withstand the wiles of the devil. For we wrestle not against flesh and blood, but against principalities, against powers, against the rulers of the darkness of this world, against spiritual wickedness in high places. Wherefore take unto you the whole armour of God, that you may be able to withstand in the evil day, and having done all, to stand.' (6:10-13.) The vision of the glory of God and the depths of life in him is vitally important; without it why should we ever try to know God at all? But it would be glib to suppose that we are at once taken into the life of transfiguration. Christian life is not an emotion experienced, or an idealism, or 'what a man does with his solitariness'; it is a whole life lived through every moment of its years to the end, in growing relationship to the whole Christ. It is still absolutely true, to quote Irenaeus, that 'The glory of God is a living man, and the life of man is the vision of God', but it is a *living* man, living a life in his own times, with all the depths that that entails. There is indeed the moment of vision, the 'moment in and out of time', but 'the rest is prayer, observance, discipline, thought and action'; 'some-

109

thing given and taken in a life-time's death in love, ardour and selfless-ness and self-surrender.' (T.S. Eliot, from 'The Dry Salvages' in *Four Quartets*.)

The depths of any living man are many and various. Certainly there is above all the depth of the mercy of God but if we are serious about that depth we shall find other depths in ourselves and it is foolish not to realise this. Many stories of the Desert Fathers, those men of 'great practical wisdom' as they were called, illustrate this. For instance, there was John the Dwarf who decided as a very young monk to serve God unceasingly and said to his brother: 'I want to live in the same security as the angels have, doing no work, but serving God without intermission,' and casting off everything he had on he went out into the desert. A week later there was a knock at the door, and a voice said, 'I am John'. But the brother replied: 'John has become an angel and is no longer among men.' Still John knocked, and in the end the brother opened the door. 'John', he said, 'angels who serve God unceasingly do not need cells; but if you are a man come and take up the long work of prayer, labour and repentance.' [3]

The depth of a lifetime

The Desert Fathers were indeed very clear about the first 'depth', that is, the depth of prayer which goes on to the end of life. One Old Man who went to live in the place where the great Antony had lived and died said to a brother who visited him: 'I came to this mountain when there began to be too many people in Scete and, finding things were quieter here, I have lived here for a short time.' The brother asked 'how long have you been here?' and the Old Man replied 'seventy-two years.' In the same spirit the holy abbot Pambo at the end of his life said: 'I go to the Lord as one who has not even made a beginning in the service of God.' Prayer in depth is as long as life.

The depth of iniquity

There are other depths that we have to discover—depths in ourselves, in other people, and in the whole of our society. And in discovering them we need to see that these are not separate depths. This is the century of two world wars, of Hiroshima, of Belsen, of unprecedented torture of body and corruption of minds. The tremendous cracks in the surface of civilised behaviour continue to be revealed, while the immense increase in communications, which we thought about earlier in a different connection, means that we are all aware of the depths of the inhumanity within man as never before. We meet these depths all the time and they can be paralysing; a stunned inability to cope with such change and such menace can produce what Alvin Toffler has recently called 'Future Shock' in his book of that title.

The depths in ourselves

What is even more alarming is that we discover the same roots of violence, frustration, despair and so on, within ourselves. Perhaps part of what we mean by 'prayer in depth' is an increase in the understanding of these depths in ourselves and in mankind so that they can be held steadily to the only thing that can redeem them—the love of God. 'No man is an island entire in himself . . . I am involved with mankind', so that when the evil in me is brought before the mercy of God a small part of mankind is also there. When we, as men and women of this torn and anguished world, come to stand before God who is our life, all creation begins through us to receive again the gift of life—and in that understanding lies the depth of intercession.

When we consider depths of these kinds it is clear that we will need many things to keep us from drowning in them. I will mention only three, and these because they are vital, not because they are all that is necessary.

Objectivity

For prayer in depth we need first of all a certain objectivity. There is so much illusion, deception and emotional content to prayer that we need a serious and disciplined asceticism of the mind in order to base ourselves not on our feelings but upon the truth of God. The Archbishop of Canterbury said recently when talking about *Godspell* and *Jesus Christ Superstar*, 'The whole Jesus demands the whole man'[4]—mind and will, as well as emotion. There are many other spirits beside the Spirit of Christ, and we need the ability to discern between them, to know what is true beyond feeling what seems nice to us. I speak very much from within the Anglican tradition when I say that this demands as much serious study of which a man is capable. Study of the Bible, of the

Fathers, of the liturgy, of doctrine, Church history, as well as the ascetic and mystical teaching of the ages. I do not mean study as a barren intellectual exercise, but as a solid basis for the right knowledge of God; the human mind needs to be transformed in order to know God and be brought into a right relationship to him. Vladimir Lossky wrote in *The Mystical Theology of the Eastern Church:* 'Far from being mutually opposed, theology and mysticism complete and support each other. One is impossible without the other. If the mystical experience is a personal working out of the content of the common faith, theology is an expression, for the profit of all, of that which can be experienced by everyone.'[5]

It is the clear ability to distinguish fact from illusion that will save us from depths of foolishness in prayer; it is the sort of objective common sense about ourselves and the truth of Christ that is the great hall-mark of the Desert. It is related that a devil appeared to one of the great Old Men saying, 'I am Gabriel'. But the Old Man said, 'Think again! You must have been sent to someone else. I have done nothing to deserve an angel.' And at once the devil vanished.

The experience of failure

Secondly, for prayer in depth we need to be ready for the experience of the depths of pain, limitation, and failure. The experience of pain is at a discount today; traditional ascetical practices are no longer valid for us, while the extremes of self-inflicted mortifications of so many of the saints seem to us perhaps hysterical and certainly unhealthy. Fr. David Knowles, writing on Becket from the depths of his knowledge of history and monasticism says: 'I would make bold to say that there has been no Christian saint of any confession who has not willingly and even voluntarily accepted physical hardship and privation either in atonement for his own faults or (in the words of St. Paul) to fill up the sufferings of Christ.'[6] Pain seems, in the experience of the saints to be related to the depths of prayer. And the same can be said of the experience of failure. Again on Becket, David Knowles has this to say about him: '. . . Great he certainly was . . . But greatness is not the characteristic adjective that either Scripture or the liturgy apply to the humanity of Christ. Strong, holy, loving, wise, stern—but not great, which implies a purely human standard of comparison.'[7] Martin Buber makes the same point in his essay 'Biblical Leadership':

'The Bible knows nothing of this intrinsic worth of success. On the contrary, when it announces a successful deed, it is in duty bound to announce with utmost detail the failure involved in the success . . . And, finally, this glorification of failure culminates in the long line of prophets whose existence is plain failure. They live in failure, failure is the breath in their nostrils, it is for them to fight and not to conquer; it is their fundamental experience . . . described by one of them . . . "He hath made my mouth like a sharp sword; and yet hath he hid me in the shadow of his hand. He hath made me a polished shaft—and yet hath he hid me in his quiver." ' [8]

This existence in the shadow, in the quiver, this being enclosed in failure, in obscurity, is very different from what is known as success in the world. And surely this is what the man who prays must expect? After all, what would a Christian success look like? A gentle, good person, never putting a foot wrong, always with the right word at the right time, kind and patient, with a sort of white light surrounding him? The only Christian success we know about for certain was not at all like that; he had 'no form nor comeliness . . . no beauty that we should desire him . . . despised and rejected of men; a man of sorrows and acquainted with grief.' (Isaiah 53:2-3.) He was betrayed by his friends, condemned by Church and State, and he died on a gallows between two thieves. That is the measure of Christian success. Once again, the Desert has the sure wisdom that distinguishes reality from illusion: A brother went to abbot Pastor and told him he had no more temptations and the abbot said: 'Go and pray to the Lord to command some struggle to be stirred up in you, for the soul is matured only in battles— the servant is not greater than his Lord.'

Steadfastness

Thirdly, the depths of prayer demand of us great steadfastness. We have 'to continue' like the apostles, 'steadfastly in the prayers and the breaking of bread', and this is of vital importance for ourselves and for the needs of our world. There is only one man who has gone down into hell, into the very limits of evil and sin, and that is the Lord Jesus, and it is only by continuing to be with Jesus that our own hells can be redeemed. 'Keep your mind in hell and despair not', was the counsel of the Staretz Silouan. We have to continue to believe that it is love and not hate that is at the heart of things, and that is what prayer in depth really means. A Vietnamese Buddhist, Thich Nhat Hanh, wrote this poem out of the horrors of the war in his country:

> Promise me, promise me this day
>> while the sun is at the zenith
>> even as they strike you down
> with a mountain of hate and violence,
> remember, brother, man is not our enemy . . .
>> Alone again, I'll go on
>> with bent head, but knowing
>> the immortality of love . . .[9]

To be able to make that affirmation in the depths of the evil of modern warfare is to be with the Lord Jesus who, in the same night in which he was betrayed, took bread and gave thanks.

Leisure for God

This refusal to hate or to despair, to continue doing the simple and practical thing, is a great part of what I mean by Eliot's 'a life-time's death in love'. And one of the essentials for this is leisure. Not leisure in the sense of idleness or spare time, but that freeing of oneself for attention to God alone which is so often crowded out by our modern busyness. If we are to be people of deep prayer we need to beware of the temptation to over-activity. A modern writer, a lay-woman, wrote this as a description of what she looked for in the clergy, but we can apply it to ourselves: 'I want them to be people . . . who refuse to compete with me in strenuousness; who are secure enough in the value of what they are doing to have time to read, and to sit and think . . . to be people who have faced loneliness and discovered how fruitful it is, who can sit still without feeling guilty, and from whom I can learn some kind of a tranquillity in a society that has almost lost the art.' (Monica Furlong.)

In this context of leisure for God it is worth quoting at length from a review by A.M. Allchin of a book called *Letters from the Desert* by Carlo Carretto:

'Carlo Carretto was a prominent activist in the Catholic Action movement in Italy. In his early forties he experienced a great crisis, a new and startling call from God. He left his life of "active usefulness" in the Church and went out into the desert, becoming a member of the Little Brothers of Jesus, convinced that "there is something much greater than human action: prayer. And that it has a power much stronger than the words of men: love."

His book is about his discoveries in those two areas of prayer and love. It is a book written out of the experience of the action of God in and through a man's life. It tells us about the conditions necessary for man to grow in prayer and in love; that is to say, to grow into the very life of God.

The conditions are not easy; plain, perhaps, but nonetheless demanding. The writer tells us things about poverty which we would rather not hear. He underlines the necessity for us to realise our own nothingness before we can begin to glimpse the majesty and mercy of God. He brings vividly before us what it means for the Little Brother to take "the last place", and to continue there. He shows us something of the astonishing prophetic powers of the life and witness of Charles de Foucauld—surely one of the greatest and most life-giving saints God has granted to the Church in this century.

Running through the whole book there is a deep and direct awareness of the meaning of contemplation. Here is the teaching of St John of the Cross, or of *The Cloud of Unknowing*, transposed into words which belong to our own day. Here is a fresh revelation of the gospel call to leave all and follow Jesus.

Above all, as the title of the book suggests, there is the fruit of the lived experience of the desert. "The great joy of the Saharan novitiate is the solitude, and the joy of solitude—silence, true silence, which penetrates everywhere and invades one's whole being... Here, living in perpetual silence, one learns to distinguish its different shades: silence of the Church, silence in one's cell, silence at work, interior silence, silence of the soul, God's silence."

In the silence man learns to let God be all and in all. In the desert night he finds the perfect "metaphor for my relationship with the Eternal: a point lost in infinite space, wrapped round by the night under the subdued light of the stars." The mystery of God in

all his greatness reaches out and enfolds the mystery of man's little-
ness. We begin to learn how to find the desert experience in us and
around us, wherever we may be.' [10]

Conclusion

When we talk about prayer in depth it sounds a very serious and
solemn thing, and so it is; but that does not mean that it is an earnest
straining after the unattainable, with a sense of guilt about enjoying
anything. On the contrary. Here is a last story from the Desert, about
the greatest of all ascetics and men of prayer, Antony the Great:
Once the abbot Antony was enjoying himself in converse with the
brothers when a hunter came upon them and disapproved. Antony said:
'Put an arrow in your bow and shoot it.' This he did. 'And another, and
another.' The hunter said: 'If I bend my bow all the time it will break.'
Abbot Antony replied: 'So it is also in the work of God. If we push
ourselves beyond measure, the brethren will soon collapse. It is right,
therefore, from time to time, to relax their efforts.'

Nevertheless, there needs to be a continuous effort from which to
relax, and so I am concluding with a further quotation from Fr. Basil
Pennington which emphasises the need for each one of us to be men
and women of prayer if there are to be Christian guides to these 'nomad
seekers' of whom I have spoken. Each one of us must work out for him
or herself what the real priorities are and each must give a personal
answer to his challenge:

'Perhaps one of the most basic and important things we can learn—or
rather be reminded of, for it is surely in our Christian monastic
tradition—is the need of spiritual masters. This is perhaps one of our
greatest lacks in this splendid hour of grace-filled renewal. We have
all too few spiritual masters to lead us, guide us, spur us on to full
Christian realisation. It is what so many are seeking today, a true
master, one who has been there and can show us the way, one in
whom we can place our confidence. So few have been willing to pay
the price, really to die and rise again in Christ, to come to that fullness of Christian maturation that can engender life. Our Roshi [the
Zen master] had spent at times from six to fourteen hours a day in
meditation for over fifty years. He is indeed a master, a spiritual
master. How can one become a deep human being, a contemplative,

not to speak of becoming a master, without spending some hours every day in the depths?' [11]

That was written by a monk for monks. A Christian living in the world is unlikely to be able to spend 'some hours every day' in the depths of prayer. All the same—from the depths of our conscience—what do we answer?

NOTES:

1 Source untraced.
2 *Monastic Exchange*, Vol. IV, No. 3, Autumn 1972.
3 The stories from the Desert used in this pamphlet are based on those in Thomas Merton's collection, *The Wisdom of the Desert*, London 1961.
4 From a lecture given at Trinity Institute in New York, January 1972.
5 London 1957, pp. 8-9.
6 From an article called 'Archbishop Thomas Becket—The Saint' published in the *Canterbury Cathedral Chronicle*, No. 65, 1970.
7 *Ibid.*
8 Essay in *Mamre* by Martin Buber, Melbourne and London, 1946, p. 52.
9 *Alone Again.* Extract from the Christmas 1972 edition of a periodical paper, 'Contemplatives for Peace', published in Arlington, Mass. U.S.A.
10 Review in the *Church Times*, 12 January 1973. Our grateful thanks are due to the Editor for permission to reprint it in this pamphlet.
   Letters from the Desert by Carlo Carretto is published by Darton, Longman and Todd in paperback at 90p.
11 See note 2 above.

Cowley Publications is a work of the Society of St. John the Evangelist, a religious community for men in the Episcopal Church. The books we publish are a significant part of our ministry, along with the work of preaching, spiritual direction, and hospitality. Our aim is to provide books that will enrich their readers' religious experience and challenge it with fresh approaches.